the MANdates

the MANdates:

25 real rules for successful gay dating

•

Dave Singleton

THREE RIVERS PRESS • NEW YORK

Published by Three Rivers Press, New York, New York.
Member of the Crown Publishing Group, a division of
Random House, Inc.

www.randomhouse.com

THREE RIVERS PRESS is a registered trademark and the Three Rivers Press colophon is a trademark of Random House, Inc.

Printed in the United States of America

Design by Kay Schuckhart/Blond on Pond

Library of Congress Cataloging-in-Publication Data

Singleton, Dave, 1961–
The mandates : 25 real rules for successful gay dating / by Dave Singleton.—1st ed.
(pbk.)
1. Gay men—United States—Social conditions.   2. Gay men—United States—Sexual behavior.   3. Dating (Social customs)—United States.
4. Etiquette for gay men—United States.   5. Gay male couples—United States.   I. Title.
HQ76.2.U5 S55 2004
646.7'7'08664—dc21   2003008793

ISBN 1-4000-4702-1

10 9 8 7 6 5 4 3 2 1

First Edition

To my mother Jan, who always wanted me to write a book
(though I don't think this is what she had in mind)

and

To Victor Lemas

Acknowledgments

IF THIS IS anything like the Grammy Awards, then I have thirty seconds in which to thank the world, God, P. Diddy, all the little people I stepped on to get this book published and, of course, Cher, before they yank me off the stage. So here goes.

Do you know how some things just seem to have a lucky star? This book was one of them, judging by the people who supported *The Mandates*.

To my agent Paula Balzer: thank you for your enthusiasm, wisdom, and the uncompromising crtical eye you apply to books as well as hats. Both the book and I are much, much better off for knowing you. Thanks also to the fantastic Sarah Lazin, as well as Hannah Slagle, of Sarah Lazin Books.

To Rachel Kahan, superstar editor: thanks for your brilliant editing, support, enthusiasm, and the priceless emails. Professionally and personally, you have been a joy to work with from the minute we met. Special thanks to the awesome team at Crown who worked so hard on *The Mandates*: Brian Belfiglio (director of publicity), Kay Schuckart (interior design), Mary Schuck (cover design), and Susan Westendorf (production editor), whose role ran the gamut from "big picture" cohesion to minutia like spelling clothing designer's names and Alanis Morisette songs correctly (Sadly, I must have some mental block).

My gratitude goes to Doug Clegg, Parker Ray (aka Ben Rogers), JR Pratts, Bruce Shenitz, Lisa Malmud, Sean O'Neill, Oscar Desierto, and the other writers, editors, designers, and publishers who offered support and insight. To David Rakoff, David Sedaris, Carrie Fisher, Bruce Vilanch, Marianne Williamson, Jill Connor Browne, and Michael Chabon: your books are where I go when the well runs dry and I need some inspiration.

Since the writing of a book is a pretty solitary business, I also want to thank a few friends who supported me and, without always knowing it, kept me company while I was writing: Suzanne Rittereiser, Paul Malmud, Mary Ann Donaghy, Christina Rudolf, Carol Nicotera-Ward, Susan Strawbridge, Liz Wilson, Margaret Rosen, Sara Meling, Karen Quinn, Liz Sorota, Frank Morgan, Gerry Valentine, Randolph Hooks, Tom Downing, Carol Monson, Michael Privitera, the O Positive Promotions chicks (Dude and Kermit, too), and Kim Repp.

I am fortunate to have a supportive family and want to thank them (especially my siblings who make me laugh all the time): Jan, Jim, Bruce, Beau, Judi, Elizabeth, Kaya, Katie, Amy, Matt, Chris, Jennifer, Lee, Libby, and my Dad, for instilling in me through osmosis a great love of words. I'd also like to thank the coolest "family-in-law"

anyone could have, including Manny, Lee, Lisa, Jennifer, Sarah, their mates, and kids.

There is no way that this book, or much else in my life, would have happened without the following people. Though I can never fully pay off my karmic debt to them for deep and eternal contributions to my life, there must be some cheap, crass way that I can try. Thanks to: Cathleen Rittereiser, My E-Pop! Partner, constant friend, and the only person who can make me laugh at obscure pop culture references at 7 A.M. in Starbucks; Abby Wilner, whose "Quarterlife Crisis" was just the start of something even greater; Jamie Levine, who gets an honorary *Mandates* award for friendship and bravery in the dating jungle; Ava Seave for your brilliance, mastery of using the "F" word as a verb, adverb, noun, and adjective, and for convincing me it was okay to "come out as funny"; Bobbi Whalen, who seriously makes Washington, D.C. a livable place for me; Bonnie Maglio, my soul mate and confidante in New York for a decade; Winn Ogden and Doug McKay for their friendship and pointing me in the right direction; Cathy Alter, a great writer and even better friend. (How many friends get their first books published at the same time?) Finally, my band of brothers in Washington and New York: Shane Harris, for supporting the plight of endangered cranberries and rare vodka, and your dazzling writing ideas; "young man/old soul" Aron Wilson; Steve Kempf ("Doris Day parking" is your birthright); Russell "You are such a _____" Schrader; Kevin Mischka, who inspires me with bold acts; James "Always true to you in my fashion" Hollander, the irrepressible, and charming Peter Pappas; and my two oldest friends who defy description, Bruce Morman and Bill McGinn.

Finally, I'd like to thank the many guys who participated in research for this book. My favorite definition of comedy is that it is "tragedy plus time." That was certainly true for some of the guys from around the country who shared their dating stories with me and inspired me with their resilience. I was fortunate enough to find many guys who are leading the way by sharing their wisdom and insight about what actually works. This is a compendium of your stories and, by sharing important aspects of your lives honestly and openly, we all get a chance to learn, laugh, relate, and move forward. That openness and honesty is a hell of a lot more than previous generations of our gay brethren had. So here's to you.

Contents

PART II
A GAY DATING PRIMER: DOS AND DON'TS
129

PART III
THE WHO, WHAT, WHERE, AND HOW
OF MEETING A GUY
139

PART IV
MARKING THE MILESTONES OF GAY DATING
165

the MANdates

Introduction

Of course, you don't know anything about gay dating until you're out there on the frontlines. I certainly didn't.

To borrow from the opening of *Great Expectations:* I was born. I lived. I came out. I started "dating," which I defined as an often slow, tedious process of getting acquainted with a variety of men. Once you meet someone who shares your attraction and interests, then you consider dating him on an increasingly intense level leading perhaps, one day, to a relationship.

But I didn't like dating back then. I didn't know what I was doing and there were no guidelines, so I hit plenty of bumps and potholes on the road to love. I soon chose "immediate serial monogamy" as my dating alternative since it felt less bumpy and more romantic. After all, you meet a guy you like, and after fifteen minutes of mutual sustained attraction, you become a couple. What's wrong with that? Didn't it work for Loretta Lynn in *Coal Miner's Daughter?* Maybe, but after a few attempts, I learned it didn't work for me. I'd jump into relationships faster than a paratrooper, then emerge from monogamist seclusion a year or two later, shake off the dust, and wonder what the hell happened when it was obvious to everyone else how mismatched my partner and I were. I'd take a break, chalk it up to fate, and start the cycle over. That's the life of a gay serial monogamist. I don't recommend it. When you jump into relationships that quickly, with only a shred of postbreakup analysis in between, you often end up with lovers whose interests, personality, values, and goals don't match yours at all.

After a therapist assured me I wasn't really a lesbian, despite my penchant for Sapphic insta-relationships (lifetime commitment by the second date, moving in with U-Haul on the third) and fierce Stevie Nicks CDs, I decided to quit making the same mistakes and dive into the dating pool.

I spent many nights at coffee houses, dinners, and movies with a variety of guys I met at parties, the gym, and work. I noticed that all my gay male friends were dating constantly, too, but spending an even greater amount of time talking about it.

I logged hours listening to tales of jerks, losers, the one who got away, the hot one at the bar last night, the one who wouldn't leave the house the next day, the one who seemed so sweet before he went into a drug-induced rage, and the one who came on strong like a hurricane and left without a trace. I'd like to say that we did *not* resemble the cast of *The Broken Hearts Club,* but, unfortunately, like them, we spent our Saturday mornings at coffee shops pouring over Friday's dates, and anticipating the three-ring dating circus that would follow on Saturday and Sunday. Sunday evening, we'd retrench with drinks and more dating rehash than a greasy-spoon diner.

What did I learn from all this?

I learned that there are 8 million gay men, and four stories.

I learned that tales of dating woe poured out before my required-and-stipulated-clearly-in-my-contract morning coffee made my eyes glaze over.

I learned how to get the most out of a "screener" drinks date in thirty minutes or less. This lopped off an hour and a half off my initial two-hour time. It was all about asking the right questions.

I learned that the Alcoholics Anonymous definition of insanity is on target: "repeating the same behavior over and over and expecting a different outcome."

Most important, I realized that the stories I was hearing were strikingly similar to my own. Like characters in an all-male cast of *Groundhog Day*, we were experiencing and doing the same things again and again. My friends and I discussed other men as if there were somehow two different species, "us" and "them," which, of course, made no sense.

Here we were, reasonably attractive gay guys with more opportunities than previous generations ever had, more places to be open, and certainly more coffee- and beer-induced "date talk" than I ever imagined. Thanks to the magic of the Internet, we quickly located gay neighborhoods, bars, and restaurants anywhere in the world, as well as found the actual men via phenomenally packed chat

rooms and increasingly popular on-line personals. Popular Web portals such as PlanetOut.com, Gay.com and AOL.com (the mother of all Internet love) became virtual one-stop shops for romance.

So with all these new ways for gay guys to meet and interact, why weren't we happier about it? Were there now too many options? An oft-repeated criticism of the nineties Information Age boom was that too many options do not, in and of themselves, improve anything. You need to learn to pay attention to commonsense guidelines so you can navigate through all those choices.

During an all-guy dinner full of laughs, empathizing head nods, impatient eye rolls, and attempts at advice for tale upon tale of dating woe, the idea for *The Mandates* came to me. Surveying this smart, attractive, and frustrated singles group, I asked myself the following question: With so many gay guys experiencing the same damn dating patterns, where were our rules?

PUTTING THE DATE
IN MANDATE

Let's do some "dating" math. There are 95 million men over the age of eighteen in the United States, according to the Census Bureau. Forty-two percent, or 40 million, of them are unmarried (27 percent have *never* been married—the really suspicious ones). That means up to 4 million of them are gay and single, if you believe the Kinsey study that claimed one in ten men are gay.

Aside from a few stray loners, celibate closet cases, and inmates, many of them are dating. But it's a sad, twisted tale of men alone in the cold, wreaking havoc on each other, and lost without dating guidelines.

Can a conscience rest with news like this? Historically, no civilized society has ever been without codes or norms for dating. From Australia to Zimbabwe, every society has rules about courtship, rules that young people absorb before they wade into the swamp of dating. But across the world, eligible gay men are still "social outlaws," a ragtag gang of hormonally driven cowboys riding into romantic battle with guns, "ammo," and no clue.

Gay men are in the early years of a new millennium with a whole new century of possibility. But it'll be a new century full of Friday nights alone at bars, hunched over computers virtually propositioning chat-room habitués, or watching television repeats of *Buffy the Vampire Slayer,* unless we learn how to put the "date" in mandate.

DATING RULES: NOT JUST FOR STRAIGHT WOMEN ANYMORE

All the single people I know (sadly, some of the married ones, too) want to date more successfully. Straight or gay, most singles want to rise from the muck and mire to win the dating game. But somehow, straight women are the only ones getting advice on how to do this.

In fact, women have been inundated with romantic rules lately. Don't call him. Don't seem desperate. Be "a creature unlike any other," whatever the hell that means. Fool the hell out of him if you want your shot at the goal, which, according to *The Rules,* is a *Leave It to Beaver* marriage with breadwinner husband, lovely children, fidelity forever, and a yellow brick road.

Thankfully, after *The Rules* came a vicious backlash. Independent women revolted at those outdated notions of how to nab a man, wrangle a ring out of him, and then ease the poor worm down the aisle. Then—surprise, surprise!—an author of *The Rules* announced her divorce after publishing a sequel of "time-tested" marriage guidelines. As I watched late-night comics have a field day with the irony, I thought to myself, "At least straight people have rules to complain about." And if we were going to have rules, what would they be? What kind of rules would work for gay people? I wouldn't want them to mirror typical straight rules. It's clear that they are no panacea for dating woes.

Dating rules, and the backlash, focused on straights, missing completely the other 10 percent of the population who endure the messy dating process. Why? Well, you can argue that openly discussed gay life is a relatively new concept. How can you examine gay dating habits and develop dating rules and goals when gay people are in a closet?

About thirty years ago at the Stonewall riots, the first martyred drag queen put her oversize high heel down, kicking off the gay rights movement (with great style and bearing I am sure). Until then, we lived in a shadowy, secret society with no distinct goals. Now, we're pioneering pilgrims of another age, but please, without the buckle shoes.

WHAT'S THE DATING GOAL FOR GAY MEN?

So three cheers and two shakes of a feathered tambourine for all this newfound dating freedom, but what the hell do we do with it now? Traditionally, marriage with children is the long-standing goal for straight relationships, as well as the benchmark for "girl gets boy" dating rules. But what's the dating goal for gay men? How could there be just one?

Gay marriage is certainly one possible goal for those with access to Amsterdam, Canada, and possibly one day New England, where ten thousand gays with rainbow rings will descend on Ben & Jerry's country, standing before each other, God, and a field of cows to say "We do."

But since marriage isn't a realistic option right now, maybe relationship-oriented gays can anticipate celebrating that all-important milestone—the first-year dating anniversary. If you measure gay relationships in dog years (seven for every one), you'll be hitting the twenty-five-year mark in no time.

If long-term commitment is your goal, you can always strive to co-invest in real estate, a much harder union to dissolve than marriage. Ask anyone who's ever bought a home with a significant other and then suffered through the traumas of a breakup. That's when the promise "till death do us part" becomes a dare.

Straight dating rules have one goal: the "together forever till death do us part" marriage vow. But that isn't the only gay dating goal. Gay men are too diverse to share one common dating goal. We are not subject to the same societal pressure for us to marry. Many of us wouldn't want to if we could.

Instead, the real goal of *The Mandates* is for men to date successfully. That means finding a man who attracts you, sustains your interest, makes you as happy as you make him, and wants the same level of dating as you.

That doesn't necessarily mean celebrating your fiftieth anniversary together surrounded by your grandchildren, though a few gay couples may be able to do that. That doesn't mean all the traditional trappings of straight rules, with their white weddings and promises of love everlasting. Rules shouldn't set you up for failure or set unrealistic expectations or promise impossible things. Life doesn't work like that. But rules for gay people can be guidelines and that's better than anything we've had.

Dating is difficult for anyone, but it's harder for gay men for a few reasons:

It's a numbers game. From a sheer numbers standpoint, the population of available men is relatively smaller for gays than straights (though if you live in Chelsea, the Castro, or Dupont Circle, my gay friend Steve argues, "You can't swing a cat by the tail without hitting ten of us").

We've had few role models. Off the top of your head, think of five current or past gay dating relationships you can point to and say, "I want that!"

There's a disproportional focus on youth and beauty. This doesn't apply to all, of course, but there's a gay culture emphasis on youth and beauty that often eclipses other important elements of a dating relationship. The gay "biological clock" is linked to aging, not ovaries.

It's a straight, straight, straight world. Almost all the romantic images we grew up with are straight, so we must reinvent romance for ourselves. That can be a slow process. The baggage that gay guys initially bring to dating—such as negative gay stereotypes we grew up with, and expectations based on what we saw in our families, society, movies, and television—gets lighter as the trip gets longer. But, despite more positive images than ever before, gays still have fewer role models on which to base our romantic interactions. Since we are pioneers, it probably takes us more time and more tries to find Mr. Right than it does the average straight. Hopefully, we figure it out before we end up gumming Jell-O during singles night at the old gay folks' home.

Matchmaking and fix–ups are a rarity. Where is your "Auntie Yenta" when you need her? In addition to a smaller gay single population, even fewer gay couples are willing to play matchmaker. And with your single gay pals, you can pretty much bet that if some hot guy comes along, they aren't likely to wrap him up as your birthday-surprise fix-up. More likely, they'll nab him if they can. Men, after all, are taught to go after what we want.

Gay men have a propensity toward dysfunc–tion. Okay, it's a broad generalization, but find me one gay man who will refute it. I am speaking more of emotional dysfunction than other kinds of dysfunction. No one would dispute that gay men in general are very functional within the community. For example, no one can gentrify a neighborhood better than we can. While there's no mistaking that gay men are functional in many ways, studies show that our community has higher instances of alcoholism, drug addiction, and self-loathing than the straight population. All of which make dating tougher, unless your dream guy is a Tennessee Williams character.

There's a wide range of dating goals. Want a challenge? In a community with such diverse dating goals, try to pinpoint the guy who wants what you want. Despite headline-catching battles for legalized gay marriage, many gay guys have zero interest in getting married. No societal pressure on gays to marry is a curse for some, but a blessing for others who relish freedom from traditional social constraints. Since a long-term relationship with a lifetime commitment isn't the only gay dating norm, you have to figure out what you want and then find an emotionally and physically compatible guy who wants the same.

SO MANY MEN, SO MANY OPTIONS, SO MUCH CONFUSION!

To paraphrase that Miguel Brown disco anthem, there are "so many men, so many options!" Options can confuse rather than focus. Based on observations from men interviewed for this book, dating goals range widely from superficial (looks, money, sex, casual hookups) to deep (common interests and companionship) to all points in between. More to the point, many guys either don't know what they want, say they want one thing but pursue something else, or are too paralyzed by options to decide on a goal.

Unless you've been cloistered in a monastery or are a recently "out" dating virgin (we call these newbies), you've encountered guys who have confused, tortured, or mysteriously abandoned you. Maybe you've even been the person re-

Introduction

sponsible for a former date's psychiatrist bills. In either case, some of these typical gay archetypes might ring a bell:

Peter Pan–sexual. As Andrew, a thirty-two-year-old Princeton grad from New Jersey who runs his own consulting business, said, "I met what I thought was the perfect guy for me. We were a good fit in every way from sexual to social, loved doing the same things, even finished each other's sentences. But, at the end of the day, he wanted to settle down, and I didn't—and still don't—want that. Nothing against it, but I just want a fun guy to hang out with and date, not move in with and settle down." Andrew wants lots of intimacy and will come on strong, but don't get too close. His little green flying suit is never far, far away.

The poetic "bait and switch" body Nazi. Bill, an athletic thirty-one-year-old from Minnesota, says, "Having a boyfriend these days is all about your body fat percentage." His idea of a perfect date is sharing one of those tasteless MET-Rx nutrition bars after a romantic "his and his" caliper test. But in his personal ad, he claims he's interested in "reading, writing poetry, long walks on the beach at night, and guys who take care of themselves emotionally as well as physically." There is no truth in this advertising.

The young, restless, and clueless. Aaron, a twenty-four-year-old bartender in Ft. Lauderdale, thinks dating is "all about money, looks, and social status. When guys see I am a bartender, they want a fling but nothing real." Aaron wants a relationship with a guy around his own age who shares common interests like music and art history, but hasn't found one who takes him seriously. Then again, most of the guys Aaron meets are older and hang out at the bar, where Aaron spends 60 percent of his free time.

Mr. Too Old to Be Looking for Love in All the Wrong Places. Kevin, a thirty-eight-year-old association executive, says, "I want a boyfriend to create a life together, not some occasional sex buddy." Though he attracts enough guys to keep his dating stream steady, the dates consistently fizzle after the first or second one. He isn't sure if he comes off too desperate or too aloof. It's dawning on him that, at his age, he might be looking for love in all the wrong places, like gay bars and clubs, but he doesn't realize that there are alternative meeting places. He's sitting home alone on Saturday nights questioning a new approach before dating anymore.

The "bi–curious" male who's as straight as a circle. Tim, a thirty-six-year-old lobbyist from Washington, D.C., wants "a guy to fool around with once in a while, somebody who's more like my straight college roommate," so Tim ends up dumping any guy who exhibits stereotypically gay characteristics from Clinique in the medicine cabinet to a fondness for dance music. He meets lots of gay guys at the gym and through work, but he's quick to point out that dating isn't satisfying. Though he can't see himself actually dating a guy, he still craves the sex long after any "curiosity" should have been satisfied. Tim is typical of many gay men who say they are bi-curious, just experimenting, or want a guy who's "straight acting," which usually just means they dislike themselves.

From the "young, restless, and clueless" to the "too old to be looking for love in all the wrong places," you'll encounter many different types of guys. One guy wants to date so he can find a life partner, the sooner the better. Another guy wants to find his match for "no strings" hookups. Many want to break bad patterns and just eliminate psychos from their comfortable, casual dating repertoire. Understand what motivates you so that you can understand what motivates him! As you learn more about yourself, and your nature, you'll understand your dates better.

Forget the psychobabble for just a minute, and face one fact: gay or straight, men are men. Successfully dating a man, when you *are* a man, takes special skills, insight, and understanding that this book aspires to provide.

So if you're gay, throw out whatever dating rules you've heard. Most make no sense for gay men since they were created to give women a leg up, so to speak, on straight men. Their success depends on a woman's ability to trick a man into total surrender and holy matrimony. The dating rules you've heard are all about gender differentiation. Not much help for you, are they?

What makes sense, however, is for gay men to learn through other gay men's dating experiences. Sharing our common "war" stories is one of the benefits from gay men coming out in droves since the 1970s. Maybe that's why I refer to *The Mandates* as "lessons learned from the frontlines of gay dating." Learning these funny and true rules will help you gain perspective on your dating goals, target your best type, weed out losers earlier, and avoid common pitfalls.

PART I

The 25 MANdates

1

LET YOUR EYES SAY EVERYTHING YOUR MOUTH SHOULDN'T– FOLLOWING THE RULES OF BODY LANGUAGE

Everyone who's ever been on a bad date (can I see a show of hands please?) knows about common body-language signs and what they mean. Crossed arms. Eyes averted. Fidgety hand movements. Bodies contorted and shifted in opposite directions, as if repellent magnetic forces were at work.

Body language can be a powerful communications tool. If you believe behavioral science studies, upwards of 80 percent of all communication is nonverbal. All you have to do is look to the animal kingdom to see how rules of attraction are acted out via body language. Male peacocks show their colorful plumes. Lions fight each other to show sheer brute strength. Wall Street brokers reach deep in their pockets to draw their American Express Gold Cards to pay for the costly pre-mating meal at Nobu.

Male and female courting rituals have always included these nonverbal signs of attraction. Awkward behavior induced by hormonal surges has affected dating traditions forever. Traditionally, men have been the pursuers, the hunters. Women have been the pursued, the selectors. Nature's explanation of this—that it is most beneficial for the continuation of the species for men to plant their seed as wide and as often as possible, and for women to be selective in choosing the strongest mates—fulfills the straight world's notion of "survival of the fittest" theory.

"Survival of the fittest" takes on a whole new approach in the gay male world—"fittest" becomes more than a metaphor. It means that those with the best faces and physiques have the greatest power. And it means that gay men, while traditionally the hunters, must find a way to be both the hunters and the hunted. Successful hunters cannot be too obvious in their pursuit. The hunted cannot be too fey in their selection. Ah, there's the rub.

To paraphrase Dr. Seuss, "Oh, the extent to which we'll go!" describes what some guys will do in their pursuit of a man. Eric, a handsome thirty-two-year-old sportswriter, developed a crush on Jess, a drop-dead handsome real estate agent, at an open house. As Eric put it, "I met this realtor, and even though I wasn't in the market yet to buy a home, I would've bought a year's supply of Barbie hair clips from this guy. I started frequenting open houses he hosted, regardless of the price range or neighborhood.

But, every time he came near me, I could barely look at him."

Jess was friendly to Eric, but businesslike. Over the next four weeks, Eric thought he was being subtle and cool by just showing up and making small talk so that if things were to develop, they'd have a chance. Sometimes he would casually ask Jess about one of the properties, which ranged from a one-bedroom in the low $100,000 range to a million-dollar town house. Other times, he would be too shy to say anything at all. Maximizing body language does not mean standing frozen like an exhibit at Madame Tussaud's. When he did speak, he fidgeted with his hands like some reject geek from a John Hughes film. And out of shyness, he often averted his eyes whenever Jess answered him directly.

Eric's "pseudo-aggressive" dating strategy didn't work. In fact, Jess the realtor is probably calling Madonna right now to get the name of her antistalking security consultant. Eric should have maximized the first meeting better through more focused eye contact and body language that showed interest, not desperation. Eric's initial efforts should have been all about getting Jess to meet him somewhere more intimate for a drink, so that he could pursue in a focused and personal setting.

Jerry, a thirty-four-year-old single stockbroker from Chicago, had a much different, more successful experience using eye contact and body language. At a bar one night, he practically bore a hole through a hot man every time

they passed each other, but the man would never look back. Every time Jerry looked at the guy, he held his gaze for a few seconds, and eventually the object of his lust started glancing back. They continued this dance for about an hour, pacing around the bar like panthers, sizing each other up from every angle amid the smoke and disco.

After a while, they were comfortable enough to be physically near each other, talking to others but with palpable sexual tension between them. They were standing closer, saying everything that needed to be said through body positioning and stance. By the time their eyes locked and they both said hello, they were already in the middle of a conversation that had begun with body language. No one had to make an awkward first move.

They exhibited the perfect attitude blend of "part hunter, part hunted, part wanting, part could-care-less" that always wins when you are on the prowl.

It's essential to maintain interest, but you don't want to come off as needy, desperate, or an immediate sure thing.

John, a thirty-nine-year-old financial analyst from Baltimore, summed up the feelings of several men I spoke with when he said, "It's hard to admit this because I sound so shallow, but as soon as you find out someone is totally interested in you, your level of interest falls a little." Maybe for men it's one of those unfortunate laws of human nature, like car wreck rubbernecking. It's definitely not helpful in streamlining dating. But that's where using body language can help.

Combat coming off as too interested by using body language to express yourself without giving away too much. Let the excitement build slowly and subtly. Unlike words, body language can rarely be used against you. No one can prove your intent. So you can maintain some mystery as you explore and initiate contact.

Given the laws of human nature, here are seven step-by-step guidelines on how to avoid crashing and burning when you are in hot pursuit:

1. Don't tell everyone what and whom you are after. You do not need the pressure of a gay cheerleading squad "rah-rahing" you on as you make your move. You are not Rocky. This isn't about crowd pleasing.

2. Cut your losses when it's clear it's going nowhere. Take Eric's example as your paradigm; if, after the fourth house, "there ain't nothing goin' on but the rent," quit stalking the poor guy and move on to greener pastures.

3. Don't use lines! To paraphrase advice my grandmother gave me, "Better to remain silent and be thought a fool than to speak up, use a tired, worn-out line on him, and remove all doubt."

4. Remember that the word desperation comes from an ancient Greek term that roughly translates to "you'll never get laid."

5. Remember the first rule of business negotiations: be willing to walk away from the table. Nothing is ever as attractive to a man as a man who is interested and interesting without an agenda.

6. The eyes have it! Once you make eye contact, you need to hold it for five seconds. Count it out in your head if this is really hard for you to do at first. But there's no way you are going to pique a man's interest by speedily averting your eyes as if you were caught cheating on an exam.

7. When it comes to body language, imagine you are Baryshnikov without the leg warmers. Use body language to your best advantage by acting as if you are a dancer of the first order. Dancers put all their emotions, feelings, and desires into self-contained movement and body language. Every glance, posture, and gesture tells a story. So when confronted with the Antonio Sabato Jr. look-alike you want to meet, you decide if you want the story to be "I want you now, I will have you, and you will love it" or "I am a complete moron incapable of even cursory, nonshaking interaction, and by the way, I am probably this awkward in bed, too." The attitude you choose is the one you'll project.

2

ALWAYS GET THE CARD–

DON'T GIVE THE CARD

(Or: At Least Control Freaks Don't Sit by the Phone Waiting)

●

You meet a desirable guy and soon sense mutual attraction. You make it through enough introductory talk to realize he is someone you'd like to know better, but for whatever reason, one or both of you needs to end the conversation. At the point where it is time to exchange information, what do you do?

There is always that awkward moment. Do you pull out a card and hand it over? Do you scribble your name on a matchbook with a pen borrowed from some bartender and slip it to your new friend before he leaves? At a party, do you write something provocative on a cocktail napkin and have it delivered by one of the caterers?

It is always best in situations like these to get the card.

Why? Three reasons:

1. It gives you a sense of mystery. It shows interest in the other person, but it makes you seem more desirable, that you are in no rush to hand over information on yourself.

2. You get the control. Were you a little buzzed at the time of the meeting? Want to decide hours later, after you have come to your senses, that Mr. Right was a martini-induced mistake, not worth a follow-up? You can, as long as you haven't given him license to find you via phone, fax, e-mail, and courier.

3. No sitting by the phone! You don't want to be, or even give off the perception of being, helplessly and passively waiting for anyone to call you.

There are advantages to restraint. There are also advantages to control. It is a good tactic to be fresh out of cards when Mr. Obnoxious just won't leave the party until he gets something, anything, with your handwriting or contact information on it. But when you are the one who wants Mr. Right's telephone number, don't put yourself in the position of waiting to be called by giving out your card.

This means that you will be the one doing the asking. Once you achieve your goal and get his card, it really doesn't matter if you give him yours or not. But if the chances that you will do something awkward are greater if you get the card, then hand yours over. For example, what if he asks you for your card first? It will be strange for you to say,

"Sorry, Charlie, no cards on me," have him give you his, and then mysteriously "find" one of yours in your left pocket.

Playing "cards" like this is a "who plays their hand first" Wild, Wild West scenario with precise timing. The stakes are high if you wait too long or get your bluff called.

Thirty-one-year-old Tony, research director for a major pharmaceutical firm, prides himself on his ability to assess a person's character. But he got really frustrated meeting men at parties and bars, giving them his card, and never hearing from them. "I knew we were hitting it off, so I offered my card because you never know how long you have to talk to someone at a cocktail party. Maybe he has other plans and has to leave, I don't know. So I wanted to be prepared. The guy would almost always smile and say he'd call, so I didn't feel the need to get his card."

But maybe Tony was too prepared. Maybe he played his hand too quickly. And as he learned from experience, he should have taken more control. When he met a guy he liked, he thought that leaving their meeting with clarity about who would call was all that was needed. Tony thought that being aggressive precluded his being the "happy to sit by the phone and wait for the call" type. Wrong.

He is now a big believer that, when it comes to the "data swap," it's more empowering for him to get the card first.

3

TELL YOUR FRIENDS
WHEN TO SHUT *THEIR*
MOUTHS FOR *YOUR*
OWN GOOD

●

When you are out carousing with friends and happen upon someone who makes your heart (and whatever else) flutter, you may find yourself suddenly back in high school, with commentary reverberating from all sides. Thanks to the gay gossip network, you may hear too many whispers in your ear about him, his life history, what he's like, and whom he's dated.

Or, worse, he may start hearing stories about you. This is when you tell friends to shut their mouths for your own good.

For instance, if your friends Bill and Gene pick up on your attraction to some new guy, they may just prop themselves next to him and start telling him stories all about you. The comments that "friends" get away with in this circumstance are nothing short of criminal.

These friends act under the guise of being your "agents," ostensibly to build you up and sell you and your attributes to the new guy. They say things with a humorous twist because, after all, they can say anything as long as it is said in humor. This is the common and heinous "B-b-but I was only joking" defense so popular among passive-aggressives everywhere.

In front of dates I barely knew, I've had "friends" jokingly point out the social faux pas I made years ago, the disastrous last relationship I had (which they laughingly referred to as Nine Minutes), and the small scar on my leg that they continued to find so fascinating.

When you spot a potential new date in social settings with friends, focus on these three truths:

1. Friends should take vows of silence like Trappist monks.

2. Friends should be like children—seen and not heard.

3. Friends should have an immediate onset of TSAD (temporary social Alzheimer's disease), in which you look familiar and they can vouch for your strong character, but they retain no recollection of any specific incident, previous boyfriend, embarrassing moment, or unpleasant physical characteristic.

Perhaps during dinner with friends, you spot a hot man at the bar. Once dinner evolves into a drink at the bar (where the eye contact investment you made with Mr. Hottie has paid off) The Mandates must take over. You have to act before your friends get the chance to dish you to high heaven. It's times like this that make you wish you'd worn your Dolce & Gabbana, rhinestone-studded "Payback's a bitch and so am I" T-shirt to keep them in check.

How do you optimize the situation and not lose the new guy?

1. Be aware of what's important here. What's important here is grabbing a few minutes alone with the prospect. You might love your friends dearly, they might be the first people you call from your honeymoon once you and the prospect hit it off, but right now they fit in like a banjo section in an orchestra.

2. Get rid of your friends if the situation warrants it. Write a note on a piece of paper and secretly slip it to the prospect. In the note, tell him that you are with a group of judgmental Mormon work colleagues, and that you are stepping outside to say good-night to them but would like to meet him back at the bar in two minutes.

3. Bring out the threat of retaliation. In a quick but clear manner, go around the table from friend to friend as the dinner is ending, reminding each one of an embarrassing event that you will mention, if forced. Paybacks are hell. Make them realize that.

THE "HURRY UP BUT HOLD BACK" FACTOR— MEN WANT WHAT *THEY* WANT WHEN *THEY* WANT IT, DON'T *WE?*

●

"**D**on't be the rusher or the rushee" is an important motto for gay guys.

Men have been conditioned from birth to want what we want when we want it. We are rewarded for asking for what we want, and for pushing to get it as quickly as possible. And in a perhaps curiously American twist, we aren't allowed to feel that great about a victory unless we have earned it.

But when a man is pursuing another man, suspicions arise if the pursuit is too fast. Watching another man try to impress you, sweep you off your feet, and go through the paces to win you over is amusing for about a minute, but can quickly deteriorate into pity if he can't get a grip on his abject enthusiasm. "For God's sake, let me earn it before you worship me" might spring to your lips. On paper, having excessive compliments paid you might sound flattering, but chances are you'll either miss your participation in the hunt or feel played as if you were the TV and he were the remote. You might well lose interest completely. But don't throw out the baby with the bathwater. See if you can save the situation. See if the man flirting with you can curb his drool long enough for reciprocated attraction. What if he's a great guy who's given in to a brief but curable siege of adolescent hormones?

First, try using some self-deprecating humor. Try to find some shared human experience, so you'll be on a more even keel. If he can laugh with you laughing at yourself, the flirtation might be salvageable.

Bill, a thirty-two-year-old pumped-up advertising executive from Boston, gets aggressive "come-ons" from guys all the time, but he hasn't learned how to respond suitably to them. Even when the guy coming on to him is attractive, Bill gets embarrassed, looks away, freezes up, and acts generally annoyed. Sometimes in response to a come-on that makes him uncomfortable, Bill squeaks out a patronizingly pat "You, too!"—one of the most predictable, flirtation-killing responses of all time. In the future, Bill should relax and respond more playfully to a "too strong come-on" by saying something like "But you really want to know my mind, right?" or "You are a little delusional. I like that in a man."

Second, try to change the subject and get the focus of attention off you (just briefly, of course). Pick a topic, start your discourse, and find out if your new fan is interested in more than just your seventeen-inch biceps. Why not cut to the chase and see if his infatuation can survive your cold but concise three-minute paraphrase of today's CNN headline news?

This works for twenty-eight-year-old hotel manager John from Dallas, who uses the "current events" bluff tactic to distract initial conversations away from awkward, premature focus on body parts. John says, "My way of dealing with new guys who only focus on the physical and start conversations with phrases like 'Great arms!' is to turn into a gay Larry King and start a discourse on world events. You find out quickly if the guy has a brain, and if he's actually interested in you as more than a slab of meat."

Finally, don't react strongly to any initial comments from a guy. Don't back off too quickly. But don't beam like the prom queen as you field compliment after compliment, either. Hesitating a little allows your object of affection to step up to the plate, realize you are nobody's pushover, and try a new approach with you.

EAGER BEAVERS
GNAW QUICKLY,
THEN DROWN

Be a Zen beaver . . . your dam will come.

I think we all like the poetic idea of a relationship evolving from a friendship that somehow catches fire. When I mention this to my gay Saturday-morning coffee klatch, after they stop laughing their asses off we all agree that this is as rare as finding the proverbial needle in the haystack.

We are hungry for a really good meal, but instead, we are the fast-food generation, expecting to see golden arches and drive-in windows along each stretch of the freeway of love. Many gay men—many men, in general—feel that romance should be fast and furious. You have a strong, immediate lusty thirst that must be quenched. And, for the majority of us with inherent male pride issues, we need to know immediately that the object of our affection wants us as well. Especially in this digital and cellular communications era, instant gratification just seems too slow.

Give it time! You don't always have to meet him and know instantly that he's the one. In fact, a sure sign that he may be the one is that sudden panic once you realize he is a serious contender. One of the downfalls of liking him is that you must then face your fears of inadequacy, intimacy, and commitment. Faced with a possible match, you naturally feel the desire to flee, heading south to the border.

Joel, a thirty-three-year-old science teacher from Long Island, says, "If he doesn't call you back for a week after you have sex, it's fifty-fifty whether he never wants to see you again or has fallen deeply in love."

When I first started dating, I thought it was important to call someone the next day if I had a really great time, especially if sex was involved. I usually said, "I had a great time, hope to see you again soon." What they'd hear was "I am so madly in love with you that I now claim all your free time as mine. Say good-bye to being single. I own you."

Gay men are like straight men in this instance. Men just take longer to process a date. Men and women define the "acceptable amount of time to call after a date" differently. For many women, an acceptable amount of time is probably a couple of days (come on, ladies, don't lie and say it's longer). For a man, it can be a week, or longer.

Sadly, some expect relationships to be linear. That is, you

meet, date a few times, fall in love, and spend all your time together. In truth, for gay men, a more workable model is that you meet, sleep together ASAP, date a few times, don't see each other for three months as you both "process" and date every man in sight to make sure you aren't missing anything, meet again by chance, date a few more times, sleep together the night before you both go on separate vacations with other friends, write a postcard here or there over the next two weeks, cancel at least three dates once you both get back, date a few more times, and a few years later—voilà, you are a gay success story with commitment ceremony, rainbow rings, and both of your mothers' silver settings newly earmarked in their wills.

Next time you are tempted to act too quickly during or after a date, remember these three "eager beaver" rules:

1. Leave an awkward moment alone. As you are ending your date, don't compulsively say, "I'll call you." It's a male "trigger gene" somehow embedded in our DNA that makes us do this. Take a moment and think about it all before saying anything. Look in his eyes and hear what he says. Then decide how you want to end the evening. Chances are, if there's no physical touching (e.g., hand holding, hand on shoulder, kiss) at this point, one or both of you might have dating doubts, in which case some distance keeps you from pushing the fledgling attraction over the edge.

2. If you don't talk to him for a week, don't get bent out of shape or assume something's wrong. Forty-two-year-old Doug from New Jersey summed up the feelings of many guys I spoke with when he said, "I ruined potentially decent romances when I ran into the guy I went out with a couple of days later and acted insulted that we hadn't spoken. Yeah, I'm sure he really wanted to call me after I pouted on the street."

3. Do not free–associate into his message machine. Practice the message first by calling from work or your cell phone and leaving it for yourself at home. I once left a date a five-minute message, in which I not only reviewed our date, but also debated the pros and cons of going out again, as if I were some modern gay Hamlet pondering whether a future date was "to be, or not to be." Needless to say, it was not to be.

ARRANGING YOUR CD SELECTION FOR THAT FIRST DATE

(Or: Limiting the "Liza" Factor)

●

Monitor the portfolio diversity in your CD selection today!

Remember that CD selection is one of those key areas, like the medicine cabinet, where actions speak louder than words as potential dates sum you up. To be brief but clear: don't have the complete collections of more than three absolutely fabulous female singers.

How many times can he count the name Liza as he scans down the list? *Liza Live at Radio City, Liza Live at Carnegie Hall, Liza Live with Mama, Liza Live without Mama, Liza's 12th Comeback Concert.* The same goes for Bette, Barbra, Cher, Patti, Diana, and those sixties retro divas Dusty and Nancy.

As you are rearranging your CD collection, remind yourself to be vigilant when referencing these divas! Stop your mouth from betraying you with tired catchphrases from these women's songs that may somehow have snuck into your everyday vocabulary. If your speech contains phrases from diva songs, such as "love hangover," "stir it up," "don't rain on my parade," "maybe this time," "it's all for you," "oops, I did it again," "if I could turn back time," and "you don't have to say you love me, just be close at hand," you must excise them with haste.

What key personality characteristics are associated with each diva? If the man you want to shag has more than three albums by any of these major divas, the following chart gives you a simple way to type a date by his music.

HOW TO TYPE HIM BY DIVA

DIVA OF CHOICE	CHARACTERISTICS
LIZA MINNELLI	Overemotional, cheery exterior hides an inner well of drama, vulnerable, a hopeless romantic with the accent on *hopeless*. Usually can be found humming "Maybe This Time" up and down the grocery aisle.
BARBRA STREISAND	Narcissist, obsessive, perfectionist. Honestly believes he is the greatest star, too. And, also like "Funny Girl," he probably does have thirty-six

DIVA OF CHOICE	CHARACTERISTICS TO EXPECT
	expressions. "Sweet as pie to tough as leather" only begins to accurately describe them.
BETTE MIDLER	Sassy, will trash you to filth when you turn your back (so much for "Friends"). Funny, though, with a comeback to send any tormentor to hell and back.
CHER	Tough, insecure, cynical, expects to be betrayed. If he could turn back time, there'd be that one who got away to whom you will constantly be compared.
DIANA ROSS	Expect demands and delusions of grandeur from this love child. Despite his humble origins, be prepared to keep a fast pace, as he adds to his china pattern and entertains on a grand scale. Ain't no mountain high enough to stop him from social climbing.
MADONNA	You better be ready to express yourself fast. You'll have to assess which specific Madonna CDs he owns to

learn which Madonna persona he has adopted, as every gay man under fifty on the planet has taken on at least one. Is he "material boy," "yoga New Age ray-of-light guy," "sleek vogue icon," "pimp daddy club guy," or "American lifer"?

JANET JACKSON

In control, but not really. Not when he's from a dysfunctional family. Will have no problem at all when you decide to get your first face-lift. Might even offer you the family group discount.

PATTI LUPONE

Desperate for attention; probably was an ADD kid. Severely needs Evita's "Casa Rosada" forum to vent his hyperconnectivity. Will find grand emotion in just about anything from noodles to the nightly news.

PATSY CLINE

Depressive, given to fits of moodiness and drinking lapses based on lunar cycles. Vacillates between feeling crazy in love with you and wanting to go walking at midnight.

Arranging Your CD Selection for That First Date

DIVA OF CHOICE	CHARACTERISTICS TO EXPECT
DUSTY SPRINGFIELD	Passive-aggressive. Not nearly as laid-back as he'd like you to think. It's constantly churning there, inside the windmills of his mind.
NANCY SINATRA	Sassy. Check under his bed to make sure his boots are carefully stashed away in a closet.
JUDY GARLAND	Addictive, manic-depressive, and moody, but unlike poor Judy, your new guy has Betty Ford as an option.
BILLIE HOLIDAY	See JUDY GARLAND and add a slew of minority-based discrimination challenges to the mix.
SADE	Too smooth, an oily operator no matter where he's from, coast to coast, L.A. to Chicago.
WHITNEY HOUSTON	He'll always love his crazy, *E! Hollywood True Story* antics. You'll always love the false image you had of him.

DIVA OF CHOICE	CHARACTERISTICS TO EXPECT
SARAH MCLACHLAN, NATALIE MERCHANT, ALANIS MORRISSETTE	A closet lesbian, but he can only hide his two cats from you for just so long. His experience with U-Hauls is a plus if things work out for you two. If he knows the words to "Angel" or "Thank You," run.
PATTI LABELLE	Wild; a potentially unhealthy attachment to bizarre hairstyles and eighties "new" attitudes.
MARIA CALLAS (OR ANY OF THE GREAT OPERA DIVAS)	You thought *La Bohème* was dramatic? The "time-honored" gay opera queen gives new meaning to the word *dramatic* on your dinner date when service is slow and the meal presentation is imperfect. You'll wish you were *La Bohème*'s dying Mimi.
BRITNEY SPEARS, CHRISTINA AGUILERA, PINK, MYA	Be on "aging twinkie" alert. If you are even discussing Britney or Christina in any context other than the gift you got your eight-year-old niece for her birthday, you are robbing the emotional cradle.

Arranging Your CD Selection for That First Date

7 | AVOIDING MATRON MEDICINE CHEST SYNDROME

You are a thirty-one-year-old man living alone in your own apartment on the outskirts of Chicago. Yet your medicine chest has enough moisturizers, night creams, day creams, midday creams, tonics, salves, lotions, potions, Retin-A, and Botox to keep a boatload of Park Avenue matrons moist and molded for a month.

What's wrong this picture?

Nothing, if your goal is getting a perfume-sprayer job at Saks. Or, if you are fast on your feet and have an empty locked drawer, you can have the best of both worlds. You can harbor your cosmetics like a fugitive, quickly throwing them into the drawer when the doorbell rings for that first date.

As Lance, a twenty-seven-year-old self-described "flannel shirts and jeans kind of guy" from Seattle, put it, "It can be a little disconcerting to meet some hot, butch-looking guy, go to his apartment, enter his bathroom, and discover colored jars of stuff on the counter labeled "dramatically different moisturizer," "Beauty Lab's soothing and firming fine line serum," "Bienfait Totale," and "honeybee kissable lip balm."

As Seinfeld would say, "Not that there's anything wrong with that." But don't waste your time trying to pull off a "superstud natural man" persona when your bathroom toiletries selection looks like an Aveda salon.

In general, do you want to date your grandmother or a man with her nighttime beauty regime? No, I didn't think so. So why would he?

Here's what should be in your medicine chest:

- One can of "drugstore bought" shaving cream. (If you must have a brand name, Gillette is okay.)

- Crest toothpaste (the bleach you just bought from your dentist should be hidden away).

- One toothbrush (leave all the others you bought "just in case" for overnight guests stashed away under the sink).

- One wood-handled, manly, painful porcupine-bristle hairbrush.

- One can of nondesigner gel or hair cream (but just one, and no spray or mousse).

- An old-fashioned, leather, masculine toiletry kit with nail clipper, just like Dad had.

- One cologne, which can be your choice, but only display one. Do not display every colored cologne bottle you ever received on top of the commode, unless you are auditioning for the role of "older gay neighbor" on *That '70s Show.*

- One bar of Irish Spring soap (no Camay or Dove).

- One economy-size moisturizer (shows manly concern for value over vanity). You don't want to end up looking like crinkled, aging icon Robert Redford. There has to be a middle ground.

Any product with a Clinique, Estée Lauder, Aramis, Calvin, or other designer brand name should be tucked safely away. Any Kiehl's products should be removed from the bathroom altogether. The "banned" list includes eye cream in the refrigerator, anything from France, and the "Auntie Mame" puffy-eye pack in the freezer.

KEEPING THE MISTER
IN MYSTERY

There is incest in the gay community, and more than just what you hear discussed in twelve-step group meetings at the Gay Community Center. I am talking about the kind of social incest that results from years of seeing the same faces over and over, dating a few of them, and slandering the rest. In a jungle like this, you need to be guided through the murky crowd by an inner voice of strength. I like to call this Accessing Your Higher PR Person.

Here are some warning signs that you have less mystery than an episode of *Diagnosis Murder:*

- You say things like "I need to meet a new man" at least once a week to the same three friends, all of whom you have dated at some point in the past five years.

- You meet a new guy by chance when you're running in the park. He invites you to a party. You are thrilled because finally you'll get to meet some new faces. You'll get to reinvent yourself, be the guy you have wanted to morph into, but have been held back by those pesky friends who think they know you. You go to the party looking fierce, walk in the door, and hear four shouts of "Hey, girlfriend, look at you," followed by a whispered "He must have bought those shoes today because he wasn't wearing them at lunch."

- You overhear a group of lesbians talking about your group of friends, shaking their heads and pondering how *you guys* manage such complicated interpersonal and incestuous relationships.

At this point, pray to the great Greta Garbo to have her spirit grace you with all the mystery of a movie star. For example, if you are Jodie Foster or Tom Cruise, do you go out in public without your own Pat Kingsley, famed personal publicist to the stars?

Absolutely not.

So, just because a personal publicist's fees might be out of your monthly budget range, you still need to think like a publicist when it comes to dating, because gay circles are small. You'll want your name in the news occasionally, but out of the news frequently.

If you are seen at the same bar with the same rowdy

queens, drinking and hooting and throwing things at cute boys, do you think gay men watching you will somehow understand that you are not really like that? Do you imagine that they'll see through this shallow veneer to your deep inner well?

Forget it. This isn't *Fantasy Island.* It doesn't work that way. You have a greater chance of being hit by a stray bullet at the nightly Disney parade than you do of changing your social reputation once you've been typecast by gay men.

Avoid being typed as much as you can by changing your schedule around, mixing up your crowd, and varying the places where you hang your party hat. Retain some air of mystery. Don't be the man everyone has slept with, as popular as that might make you think you are, as you slink your "touchy-feely" way through the bar, saying hi to this one and that one. Don't spread too much gossip. You can't throw mud without somehow getting some on yourself. Don't meet every man in town. Leave some for later.

Thirty-nine-year-old New York architect Bruce feels strongly about maintaining mystery on a first date. "I kind of give that Jackie O vibe—aloof yet seductive," says Bruce. "Oddly enough, the more I'm interested in a new man, the more aloof I am. Initially, don't give them too much, literally and figuratively, if you want to keep dating."

This is not to say Bruce isn't friendly, fun, and engaging. He just keeps some distance, and guys don't feel after a couple of dates that they know everything about him.

I am not saying you should lie or make things up, but what's wrong with keeping some parts of your life mysteriously hidden, as long as those things are not destructive? If you forgo mystery and send him your résumé, a press release on your life, or act as socially ubiquitous as a summer firefly, just wait for the yawn that will come once he thinks he knows all about you.

When you finally do meet *him*, the man you have been waiting for, you want as little social baggage as possible. When, after that amazing first two weeks you spend together, he tells his friends that he has met the guy of his dreams—i.e., you—the last thing you want him hearing is "You're dating that mean old queen? She dished me to filth once at Darren's beach-hat party" or "You're dating him? Did you know he dated Curtis right when he was breaking with Jonathan, and then dumped him for Randy?"

There's only one alternative to radically modifying your own behavior to maintain an air of mystery: keep a bodacious diary on everyone else's naughty habits for blackmail purposes. But you better be sure you have some mighty good dirt if you choose this option. Staying home a night or two a week might be simpler.

9

ASK AND YE SHALL HEAR!

Ask and ye shall hear, presumably, more than you'd need to know. Before you can buy that home, raise that dog, or have Mom spend the weekend with the two of you, basking in your gay wedded bliss, you need to find out the answer to a *big* question.

Is he single? Really single?

Because with men, sometimes the word *single** gets misconstrued. As in "on-line" single, a relatively new Internet

---

* Sorry to have to spell this out, but gay men seem to have a hard time understanding what "single" means. "Truly, honestly single" means that he meets the following criteria:

- He's not living with a man with whom he is sleeping in any sexual way whatsoever. No, the Bill Clinton definition of "sexual relations" does not count.
- His "ex" was informed that they have, in fact, broken up. A letter sitting on the desk waiting to be sent does not count. A well-intended plan to tell the ex soon does not count, either.
- Though chances are he's dating other people, he isn't in a monogamous agreement of any sort with anyone, anywhere.
- In case he's cohabiting in an open relationship, he doesn't consider himself to be seriously dating as he defines "serious."

phenomenon wherein the marriage vows are void once you log on to the computer. Is he "for the weekend" single, because his lover and brand-new golden retriever are spending two days away at pet training? Is he "understanding" single since he and his partner have an "understanding"? Is he "newly" single, out of a long-term relationship for a whole day? Is he "fighting" single because of the fight he and his lover had two hours ago? Or is he really, truly, honestly single? The challenge is sifting through the fairy dust of his "spin" to ascertain the real truth.

Here are the basic questions you need answers to before you can be fairly certain that he is worthy of your dating time and attention:

FRIENDS

Who are his long-term friends? E.g., are his best friends a group of club kids he met last Thursday at Sound Factory Bar?

SOCIAL LIFE

What's his average day like? When does it start, when does it end?

Don't ask him what he likes to do in his spare time. Ask him what he's done for fun in the last month, especially on the weekends. It's a more disarming way of getting at the truth, not what he'd tell you is the truth. Actions speak louder than words.

How many bartenders does he know by name around town?

Is *ecstasy* the word he uses to describe being around you, or that little white pill you see him popping?

FAMILY

What's his family like? What kind of emotional family baggage will you be inheriting?

How often does he speak with them?

Do they know he's gay?

LIFE

What are his goals—financial, personal, career?

If you give credence to personality testing, did he take the Myers-Briggs test? Which of the sixteen personality types is he? (Then quickly check to see if yours is compatible with his. An ENTJ with an ISFP is certain death.)

What's his idea of a perfect day?

LOVE

Has he been in longer-term relationships (six months to one year minimum)? In theory at least, does he like them?

What are the qualities he looks for in a guy?

How does he define a serious dating relationship?

What are the stories about his past lovers—what happened? What does he want that he didn't have before? What would he do differently next time? Do you want the same things?

Was he ever jailed for maiming, murdering, or stalking any former dates?

Ask and Ye Shall Hear!

10

HE OPENED HIS MOUTH AND HIS PURSE FELL OUT

(Or: Everything You Need to Know You Can Know in the First Five Minutes)

Perhaps the point of dating (if you are in fact reading this book for any other reason than coercion) is to, as Thoreau said, "simplify, simplify."

But then again, if Thoreau really knew what he was talking about, would he have told us to "simplify" twice?

Anyone who says that life is all about "living in the moment" has obviously not been on more than two dates anytime within the past ten years. There is a goal, a destination, for this journey. There just has to be. How else can you justify slogging through dinner after dinner, party after party, with a string of men best summed up as the bottom of the food chain?

The point of dating for many gay guys, once you pass the initial thrill (which, for gay men, often occurs later than for straight men due to "coming out" delays), is to find a compatible mate.

Some say that it takes a long time to get to know a person.

The Mandates says that everything you need to know about him, you can learn in the first five minutes. Oh, sure, the details don't come out until much later. If it's a long-lasting, positive relationship, hopefully you always learn new things about the man who becomes your life partner.

But, it is not cruel to be discerning. Of course, you have to watch that tendency toward stray judgments. He could be a really great guy, and worth a chance, even if he accidentally forgets that you were supposed to meet tonight, not next Thursday. But, on the other hand, if during dinner he leaves more than three times to check his answering machine, talks bitterly about past lovers, carries wads of cash and has no credit cards or picture ID, or speaks fondly of getting married and a green card in the same breath, then chances are you should immediately rollerblade for cover.

In many cases, all you have to do is look at him silently for a minute or two, and like a criminal who can't take the pressure, he will blurt out all his sins, fears, and dysfunctions. Time it when he does. Look at your watch and wait five minutes. You'll be amazed at the sheer raw data he'll provide. Now you know what Catholic priests have known for years: only on the rarest occasions does any confession last more than five minutes.

He will tell you about the lover who he knew had more parole violations than Amy Fisher, a sixth-grade education, misspelled tattoos, and a bad habit of petty theft. Still, he chose to let the loser move in with him.

You'll hear about his conflict between longing for a committed, fulfilling relationship and that nagging inability to be sexually aroused by anyone other than a stranger wearing a leather mask.

James, a twenty-seven-year-old music publicist in Los Angeles, calls this the "he opened his mouth and his purse fell out" syndrome. Beware TMI (too much information) early on.

As Fran Lebowitz once said, "Spilling your guts is as attractive as it sounds." And though true, the really dangerous guy is the one who seems perfect on the surface. Or, as my mother puts it, the "good package" man, the guy who knows how to sell "normal."

But a glimpse at the real core of any guy can be yours right away. Master these basic questions and dating becomes as streamlined and efficient as Martha Stewart's kitchen.

QUESTION	WHAT HE SAYS	*THE 25 MANDATES* TRANSLATION: WHAT IT REALLY MEANS
What do you do?	I'm in a new phase of my career.	I have no clue what I'm doing.
	I switched jobs.	They fired my ass.
Do you like your job?	Well, not really. Lately it's been bad for me. My boss stinks.	You will have to listen to him bitch about work every day, rain or shine, for at least six months. Worth it?
Are you out at work?	Yes, to one guy who works on an-other floor.	I am a total closet case, only one small step shy of having a fake wife-and-kids photo on my desk.
	I think so, I mean I don't hide it. I am sure people know.	I am quieter than a church mouse during Easter ser-vice. When the talk at work turns personal, I turn into a "gay male Helen Keller."

QUESTION	WHAT HE SAYS	*THE 25 MANDATES* TRANSLATION: WHAT IT REALLY MEANS
Are you out to your family?	Yes, to my sister.	Well, I told her I thought everyone was partly bisexual.
	Yes, to all, and they are coming to terms with it.	Yes, and it is a source of constant torture and discussion, which you can now be part of. P.S. My parents hate and blame you already.
	Yes, I am out to them. It's important to be honest but I can't say it's been easy for them or me. But it's getting better.	Bingo! He's made the attempt, he values honesty, but he's realistic and he's not painting a perfect picture.

QUESTION	WHAT HE SAYS	THE 25 MANDATES TRANSLATION: WHAT IT REALLY MEANS
Are you out to anyone, anywhere, other than maybe me?	No, because . . .	Being gay is bad. I am bad. You are bad. Talking with you is bad.
	It's a long story.	No, it's a short story; it's just been going on a long time.
Do you talk to your ex?	Only occasionally. It's not like we're friends and regularly communicate.	Yes, when I'm desperate for sex and/or money.
	Sure. We were together for ten years, and when our romantic relationship started fizzling after the eighth year, we found we just have more of a friendship.	If they were together that long and took that long to break up, it's doubtful they'll revert to some brief outburst of animal lust and threaten your burgeoning

QUESTION	WHAT HE SAYS	*THE 25 MANDATES* TRANSLATION: WHAT IT REALLY MEANS
		romance. But let's hope you like the guy. If things with your date go well, sounds like you'll be spending time with the ex.
	No, never, I still don't know what happened really.	And because of his callous rejection, I have more wounds than the War of 1812.
	No. Never. Could care less.	I'm a mess, I'm a mess, I'm a mess.
	I mean, sometimes I wonder what he's doing right now, that bastard! But in general? No.	I'm a mess, I'm a mess, I'm a mess.

QUESTION	WHAT HE SAYS	*THE 25 MANDATES* TRANSLATION: WHAT IT REALLY MEANS
What's his idea of the perfect guy?	Stable.	Translate: he's not.
	Smart and fun.	Translate: dumb and cute.
	Hung like a Triple Crown winner.	Translate: makes former President Clinton look chaste.
	I don't think there is such a thing. I want a smart, funny, attractive, compatible guy. Who doesn't?	Good answer! This question assesses his expectations. Are they reasonable? You want to know that he's not on cloud nine.
Are you relationship-oriented?	For the most part, yes.	Yes, I am on Tuesdays if it rains, as long as a hot piece of ass doesn't walk by.

QUESTION	WHAT HE SAYS	*THE 25 MANDATES* TRANSLATION: WHAT IT REALLY MEANS
	I am happy being single, but settling down with the right guy in a healthy relationship would be great.	This is one of those areas where it's important to qualify why you are pro or con. Your reasons why make all the difference between sounding sensible or desperate.
Did you add the word *von* to your last name before or after you moved here from Europe?	It was always there . . . After.	I am stupid, therefore I am. Applaud his sense of humor and honesty about his appalling reinvention as a Eurotrash prince.

QUESTION	WHAT HE SAYS	*THE 25 MANDATES* TRANSLATION: WHAT IT REALLY MEANS
How did your last relationship end?	I wanted more sexual adventure than he did.	He didn't rope and tie me like a prize bull at a rodeo, damn his cowboy hide.
	It's a long story.	No, it's actually a short story. It's just been going on a long time.
	It's complicated˙	But not as complicated as I am and will always be.
Do you get along with your family?	They are my best friends and very protective of me.	I have a better chance of being killed during a random road-rage incident than I do of having my family accept my boyfriend.

QUESTION	WHAT HE SAYS	*THE 25 MANDATES TRANSLATION: WHAT IT REALLY MEANS*
	We are close, with our differences from time to time. Bottom line, I know they want the best for me.	Okay, you have a chance of acceptance.
What made you declare bankruptcy for the second time?	It's a great way to clear debt and start again. I feel so great that I am starting over!	I'm a mess, I'm a mess, I'm a mess.
Why do you only carry cash?	Convenience.	Cash is untraceable. And that's a good thing when you run a global drug cartel like I do.

QUESTION	WHAT HE SAYS	*THE 25 MANDATES* TRANSLATION: WHAT IT REALLY MEANS
How come all of your friends that I've met have known you for less than six months?	Sadly, they all had to move away.	Yeah, down the street. And changed their number so I couldn't get it. But the restraining order against me can't last forever, can it?
Do you do drugs?	No! A quaalude now and then, maybe . . . and a joint on occasion, yes. But I only do these with a martini if it's offered.	"Hello, Betty Ford?"
Did it hurt to get pierced there?	No, not at all.	But it hurts like hell now and sometimes oozes.

NO ONE EVER *LEARNED* TO LOVE ANYONE, EVER... MOVE ON!

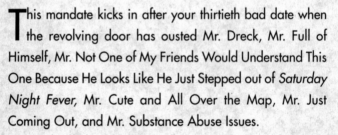

This mandate kicks in after your thirtieth bad date when the revolving door has ousted Mr. Dreck, Mr. Full of Himself, Mr. Not One of My Friends Would Understand This One Because He Looks Like He Just Stepped out of *Saturday Night Fever,* Mr. Cute and All Over the Map, Mr. Just Coming Out, and Mr. Substance Abuse Issues.

Dr. Elisabeth Kübler-Ross, bereavement specialist, calls this your "compromise bargaining" stage, when you fall to your knees and throw yourself on the mercy of the higher power.

You yell heavenward, "Just give me a man who is employed or imminently employable, doesn't scare children, is remotely attractive—to someone somewhere—and is desirous of the kind of stability that I crave. I promise I'll like him as is, even if we have less chemistry than a fifth-grade science class."

The thing to remember about this stage, when a viable candidate who "looks good on paper"* suddenly appears on the scene, is that no one ever *learned* to love anyone, ever—so move on.

Do not settle. Spare yourself the time and trouble. It will not work. Because if you have made it to the stage where you are reading this, it probably means you have inner standards that have survived your lonely periods, early coming-out years, and bad dates, making you a much stronger, tougher critic than you give yourself credit for. When you have reached this stage, you are ready, able, and willing to handle all twenty-five Mandates.

Believe me, I tried to settle a couple of times with a "looks good on paper" guy. Once, when I was twenty-seven, my handsome, well-educated gym buddy Don was in love with me. My friends and family liked him, we enjoyed the same social activities, and—this is key for any relationship to work for longer than three months—he accepted my life and me just as they were. I don't know if it was bad timing when we met, or if we were star-crossed, but I could not

---

*"Looks good on paper" refers to the puzzling phenomenon of smart, physically attractive guys with good credentials such as education and employment who, for whatever reason, aren't attractive to you at all. You can analyze to death the possible reasons for this as you rock back and forth crying, "Why?" But you still won't want to jump their bones.

make myself attracted to him. I would look at his picture before a date, remember all the times I'd seen him after swim practice, looking buff and dripping wet in his Speedo. Yet when we were on a date, I couldn't stand the thought of touching him. One night I decided that it was my fault, I had let our friendship get in the way of true love, and that we just needed a boost to cross that physical barrier. So I bought two bottles of Veuve Clicquot champagne, thinking that drinking would get me over the hump, and invited him over. On my rooftop deck, two bottles of champagne and several beers later, I was buzzed and still didn't want him. That was my waterloo. If I didn't want this hot guy on a moonlit rooftop during a warm spring night, then it wasn't ever going to happen. Fate patiently waited for me to stop trying so damn hard.

When you are faced with a man who, after three dates, leaves you colder than a trip to Baskin-Robbins, accept that this is platonic. And then help him accept it. Look him in the eye kindly but firmly, access your inner Audrey Hepburn and then utter her immortal line to Cary Grant in the film *Charade:* "Date you? No, it's not possible." If he persists with his mission and throws the "Can't we at least be friends?" option at you, finish Audrey's line by removing your sunglasses and stating sweetly and simply, "I can't possibly have any more friends. I'll let you know when one dies."

12

THE DIFFERENCE BETWEEN MR. RIGHT AND MR. RIGHT NOW: LEARN IT!

●

There is one set of rules for tricks. And one set of rules for potential relationships. And never the twain will meet.

Joe, a thirty-five-year-old doctor in New York, insists he is a "regular kind of guy, looking for a boyfriend. Why is that so hard to find?" Joe went out dancing one Saturday night at the gay club Roxy in Manhattan, where he met Phil, a twenty-eight-year-old accountant. Phil apparently found relief from the humdrum, number-crunching, nine-to-five grind in the weekend whirl of clubbing, nylon-mesh muscle shirts, and ecstasy, which he popped like popcorn the night he met Joe.

After dancing for an hour, they went home together and had wild sex. By 5 A.M., Joe was exhausted, in love, and couldn't wait for the next "date" with Phil.

The date didn't happen; Phil had left his phone number

but never returned calls. But they did see each other at parties and clubs over the next few months. Phil always greeted Joe with a friendly, familiar hug and squeeze, and on several occasions, they went home together again. The same pattern repeated—great sex, a good time, mumbled talk about getting together again, Joe would call, and Phil wouldn't call back.

Joe was left wondering why they weren't seeing each other during the week, planning dates, and going away on weekends together upstate.

Phil was trying to figure out whether the creatine he drank was giving him leaner body mass, how to lessen postecstasy depressions, and whether he was going to get invited to the Fire Island A-list parties.

The phrase "Physician, heal thyself" comes to mind.

Phil wasn't just a little absentminded, playing hard to get, or taking things slowly so romance could develop, as Joe led himself to believe. Phil was a trick who had been turned into a "repeat trick," which is not to be confused with a boyfriend.

Buddhist doctrines state that all pain in life is caused by attachment. I would add that dating pain is caused by attachment to the idea that tricks can be turned into marriage and vice versa.

The rules for fooling around are simple:

1. Keep it light.

2. Keep it fun.

3. Have no huge expectations.

4. Play it a little cool.

5. Don't ask too many questions.

6. Give yourself a reality check. Don't think for one millisecond that just because he seemed "really, really nice" when you met him at 3 A.M. in the bar, followed by a hot time together at your house at four, that somehow this guy will become, by noon, the adopted father of that Romanian orphan you've always wanted to raise with the man you love.

The qualifications for Mr. Right will, of course, vary from man to man. You might prefer a tall, dark, and handsome extrovert with brown hair who wants to run for mayor. Someone else wants a short, blond introvert who likes quiet nights home alone together. The details don't really matter. The important thing is that you'll have a good idea who Mr. Right is by how you feel when you are around him.

Do you feel safe? Do you trust him? Do you have a sense of ease? Does he reinforce you in positive ways? Are you compatible when it comes to sharing space and spending time together?

Alex met his Mr. Right, Tony, at a gay event in Los Angeles. As Alex tells it, "I was dragged to speed dating. I thought it would be full of desperate, boring guys." Tony pipes in, "It mostly was. The moderator called us all to order in a circle of metal folding chairs. I felt like was in AA.

Hi, I'm Tony, and I'm a date-a-holic." At first glance, speed dating hardly seemed to offer the hope of a Mr. Right Now, let alone a Mr. Right.

Alex and Tony made their seven-minute rounds, punctuated by the moderator clapping his hands in exasperation, saying things like "Just take any seat, boys. It doesn't matter, it's not like tops in one row, bottoms in another."

"It got to the point where I literally didn't think I could move my dry lips to form a smile one more time," said Alex. "I sat there planning escape strategies. Mr. Moderator would have to break it to my 'matches' that I had to suddenly return to my homeland, Fiji. Family tragedy, you know."

But then Alex and Tony sat face-to-face. They broke out into immediate, conspiratorial smiles. Tony said, "We just started talking, sort of laughing at the whole setup. I felt at ease with Alex. Before, I was so worried about how I looked, how everyone else looked, if I was being judged, how I would make conversation, and how I would avoid feeling awkward. I felt a genuine mutual interest with Alex, not predicated just on looks. The time flew when we talked. I wanted to tell him everything. We've been dating nine months and I still feel the same. When I was on the hunt, I always felt uneasy. That's the difference with Alex. I feel like I am with my friend."

Of all the dating couples interviewed for this book, most cited that sense of ease and compatibility as the biggest determinant of Mr. Right versus Mr. Right Now.

13

THINGS YOU SHOULD
NEVER, EVER, FOR
ANY REASON SAY OUT
LOUD TO ANOTHER LIVING
SOUL IN THE FIRST SIX
MONTHS OF DATING

●

You meet a great guy, start dating, and see green lights down the relationship road. All the checkpoints along the way have been cleared: he's single, attractive, and interested in the same level of dating as you. After one week, your guard is down and you feel that you can say anything you want to him. In a word, don't.

Words are the Pandora's box of dating. You cannot take back words once they've been uttered. Of course, you want to say and hear all the right words that will alleviate the insecurities, questions, and fear inherent in any new dating relationship. But jumping the gun with overly intimate words and actions can backfire!

Bill, a thirty-three-year-old retail store manager in Maryland, met Chris, a thirty-five-year-old businessman, at a mutual friend's birthday party. Party attendees noticed how in sync Bill and Chris were, and the two started dating with a vengeance. After two dinner dates, Bill and Chris had pretty much planned the next eight weekends together. Everything was going great until the fourth weekend, the out-of-town wedding of Bill's sister. Bill said, "Everyone will be there, it's a great time to introduce you. I never brought a guy home before." Flattered by Bill's invitation, Chris accepted.

Bill and Chris might as well have worn flowing gay rainbow flags for all the stares they got at the Georgia Baptist church wedding. Bill's family was tense because they were meeting Bill's gay boyfriend in the midst of their three hundred nearest and dearest. The tension translated to Bill and Chris, who now defined hell as being landlocked together amid Bible-thumping, poorly dressed homophobes, riddled with insecurities about their budding relationship, and stuck listening to endless streams of "straights-only" wedding talk. They broke up soon after the trip, attributing the downfall to excessive pressure.

In retrospect, they learned an important lesson. Don't speak too soon and find yourself in situations that, while tough for any couple, are impossible for a new gay couple. Don't underestimate the stress involved in demanding activities such as meeting parents, family, and friends, visiting hometowns, and attending weddings. In the first few months of dating, be careful what you say, where you go together, and what you promise.

The things you should never, ever, for any reason say out loud to another living soul in the first six months of dating are:

TO HIM

I'll love you forever.

This is it. I just know.

It doesn't matter to me what my friends think when they meet you. They'll love you.

Your HIV status doesn't make a difference to me at all.

At the bathhouse last night, I ran into a guy who reminded me of you.

Maybe we should just move in together. Things are going so well.

I'd love to meet your parents.

What's the big deal? It's just meeting my mother. She likes everyone.

I have this wedding I'd like you to go to with me.

Oh, no, I don't mind at all when you leave the cap off the toothpaste.

Since we agreed to be monogamous, it's okay to do anything we want sexually, right?

TO ANYONE ELSE

He's perfect.

He needed to borrow fifteen hundred dollars. Of course I gave him a loan.

So he spends entire weekends alone with his ex-boyfriend—so what? I think it's nice they're friends.

Do you think he's right for me?

We just know each other so well. We have no secrets.

I'm so flattered and honored that he wants us to share one checking account.

It's not that he doesn't want to see me, it's that he just needs a little more space for him on weekends so that he can focus on me when he's with me.

He just drinks that much because he's under a lot of stress right now.

He wasn't cruising that other guy. He's just naturally flirtatious.

HIT ON SOMEONE YOUR OWN SIZE

(And Double Your Wardrobe)

●

Face it. Sharing clothes is a bonus. And as Pearl Bailey said (or *should* have said), "Honey, I've had big and I've had small, and same size is better." Just make sure he has good taste.

You do not want to tumble off your tasteful perch and end up on a downward spiral. You must avoid a fashion free fall from which your only option is picking yourself up, dusting off those Sergio Valente jeans and bad jewelry, and starting all over again.

You don't want the man who lives for the postcards from Nordstrom announcing their 75 percent off sale. Nor do you want the guy who makes statements like "Oh, I only wear Giancarlo Ferre—his draping fabrics from Turkey cement my signature look."

You need to find a guy who buys from the same three clothing stores as you. If you are Banana Republic, Abercrombie & Fitch, and Kenneth Cole, and he is Eddie Bauer, Sears, and the Burlington Coat Factory, chances for your longevity as a couple are not promising.

"It's not like I'd ever make sharing clothes a major criterion of dating," said Jay, a twenty-four-year-old salesman trainee from Connecticut, "but it's definitely a perk."

It's a perk that guys don't take advantage of enough. While God blesses the "Saint Bernard and Chihuahua" couple combinations that you see all too often, such as the five-foot-one dude with the six-foot-three hulk, you have to admit it's poor planning. Both may be beefy and built, but a T-shirt for one is a leg warmer for the other. Where's the clothes-sharing potential in that combination? How do you double your wardrobe without spending a dime? There are few advantages to a gay relationship. Access to a larger selection of fine attire is chief among them.

Find a man within a couple of inches of yourself from all angles. Try to vary the hair color so you don't look like frosted twins, because who wants to look like Ken and Ken sans Barbie out for the evening? But keep the clothes all in the family. It's one of your inalienable gay rights.

15

MEETING HIS FRIENDS: THE ULTIMATE CORPORATE MERGER

●

Meeting his friends requires major strategic planning, just like a corporate merger. It will take time and research and cannot be accomplished with any valid rate of success within the first three months of dating. You need to know the players, understand their roles, respect the power hierarchy, and set a realistic two-year time plan for those friends you are targeting for early retirement, downsizing, and transfers.

It's a common misconception that your single friends are just dying to see you happily dating, coupled, or married off. Maybe not so surprising is that a few of his single friends may not want him happily dating, coupled, or married off, either. He may not be aware of this. That's why you have to be smart enough for both of you when it comes to managing friends, his and yours.

The truth is that sometimes you don't realize who your real friends are, or what you need in a friend, until a dating relationship comes along to challenge those friendship dynamics.

When I was thirty-two, it dawned on me that several of my so-called friends seemed to go out of their way to sabotage my dating relationships. Whether the sabotage was excluding the new guy from conversations or bending his ear with inappropriate information about my past or pointedly not inviting him to social functions, I realized that these so-called friends didn't want me to date anyone more than once or twice. It was too threatening to them.

At first I didn't believe it. Surely, people who supposedly cared about me wanted me to be happy. I remember introducing Karl, who became my long-term boyfriend, to a group of friends at a restaurant in the West Village of New York City. These friends drank like fishes, told stupid tales of youthful indiscretions, brought up bad former relationships I'd been in, and asked Karl and me inappropriate sexual questions about our still-forming relationship. Karl was stunned. I was like Glenn Close in the film *Jagged Edge*. In the film, she can't believe that Jeff Bridges wants to kill her, and I couldn't believe my friends were trying to kill my relationship. Glenn finally had her "typewriter" meltdown, the moment where she realized that Jeff was indeed the killer. And I had my moment when I realized that some of my friends were killers, too, and confronted them. Actually, a couple of them needed an exorcist more than a confrontation, but that's beside the point. The damage was already done.

You should be aware of his friends' reaction to you, and your friends' reaction to him. You need to know the different rules for meeting his friends versus meeting your friends.

The Mandates approach to meeting and managing *your* friends is as follows:

1. Control the environment. You pick the place to meet, somewhere where you know you'll all be comfortable, where the conversation will flow without your having to shout above the noisy crowd. One of the first rules of public relations is to never take a client anywhere you haven't been before. You don't want any surprises on a first meeting.

2. Choose the first few friends carefully. For the first meeting, invite only those friends with whom you feel truly close. Forgo that new guy who's really, really fun but a bit of a wild card. And don't invite an entire social group. Keep it small and intimate; you want the meeting to be cozy.

3. Relax! Dogs smell fear. Don't worry about the planning and organizing to the extent that you forget to have fun. If you are tense, you will set the tone for the whole evening. Set up the meeting as best you can, then relax.

4. Keep him at the epicenter. This evening is all about him, and the two of you. It's not a college reunion where you sit around reminiscing with old pals, or a catch-up session with your buddies. Only discuss topics that everyone can participate in, and when there are references to past events, make sure you bring your date into the conversation.

When you meet *his* friends without the "home court advantage," here's what you should do:

1. Be aware of the dynamics. Just being aware of the possible array of reactions to you is an important step. You don't want to be cynical, but you'd be naive to think that all his friends and family are waiting to welcome you with open arms. Of course, it's possible, and maybe meeting them will be friction-free. But chances are good that someone will be threatened by your presence, fearful of what it will mean, and consciously or unconsciously sabotaging.

2. Don't take anything personally. This is a good rule in general for life, but when it comes to his friends, remember that in their minds, you might be the reason that their fun and freewheeling pal is no longer available to them 24/7. They might resent you for it.

3. Make pals with the leader of his pack. Who is the alpha dog in his group of friends? Pay a little extra attention to him or her. Chances are this is the person who will rule either in favor or opposition to you, then influence the others.

4. Be patient with your guy as he handles his friends' reaction to you. If he has friends who are difficult, or not supportive of your dating relationship, I'd bet he already knows this is a problem but does not know what to do about it. You will get a lot further if you bite your lip before criticizing than you will if you start bad-mouthing his friends right off the bat.

5. When you reach a comfortable place in your dating relationship (not before a couple of months), gently point out any sabotaging behaviors from his friends. You'll have a little time and credibility under your belt, and you will slowly have amassed the evidence to then gently make your case.

16

WHEN MALE EGOS COLLIDE: MR. TITANIC, MEET MR. ICEBERG

You are a guy. Socialized and trained from birth to expect that your needs will be met in a timely fashion. You probably invest much of your identity in your job. And you internalize hurt way too much. And of all the aerobic exercise you do, you are probably most adept at "jumping to conclusions." Probably to a good techno house beat.

Even though you're gay, you are still a guy. The gay gene is not always as dominant over other character-trait genes as we might think, and remember, you are fighting what Carl Jung refers to as millions of years of male "collective unconscious"—a history of male patterns and behaviors passed down from generation to generation that then become part of our genetic makeup.

So the question is, on paper, would you want to date another you? Would you jump at the chance to date someone who has your same issues? Well?

Unfortunately, we don't live on paper or the answer might be simple. "Hell no!" you might shout in defiance. But don't forget you are fighting powerful forces of sexual chemistry and rules of attraction. Most of the men you crave will be similar to you in core ways, so accept that his traits, and yours, have advantages as well as disadvantages.

ADVANTAGES	DISADVANTAGES
HANDSOME	Looks fade
TOTALLY HUNG UP ON YOU	It's hard to sustain the initial relationship "in love" high—just ask Siegfried and Roy
AMBITIOUS	Work will come first all too often
POPULAR	Wants to hang out with his pals more than you
NOT TOO LOADED WITH BAGGAGE (ONE OR TWO CARRY–ON BAGS ARE OKAY)	His history of family mental illness kicks in at age thirty-five

ADVANTAGES	DISADVANTAGES
INDEPENDENT, STRONG–WILLED	You weren't the only guy to get the societal messages that, as a man, you should always get your way, that you are entitled to be moodier than a tube of mercury, and that you can never focus enough on work and money. He did, too
ABLE TO UNDERSTAND HOW YOU THINK	Able to understand how you think

Mike and Will, two twenty-something, ambitious business consultants at competing companies, met in East Hampton, New York, during a summer picnic. The sun was shining, they were relaxed, and their conversation led to dinner, which led to dating.

Their work schedules were similar: seventy-hour weeks, getting paged at random by clients, and when duty called, dating came to a standstill. Despite similar schedules and demands, each kept getting his ego bruised by the other's work focus. Big egos often mean big insecurities. Mike acted nonchalant when Will had to cancel a date due to a fast-approaching deadline, but bitched to his friends about it. Will felt tremendous insecurity when Mike had to work all weekend out of town. They allowed seeds of doubt to grow, which almost sank the relationship. After about three months, they finally let down their guards and talked honestly about their insecurities that arose from work issues. Solid negotiators that they are, they set up the following agreement to manage work overload:

- He who breaks the date for work must reschedule with something exciting, like dinner at a top restaurant or concert tickets.

- When work schedules result in changed plans, both parties agree to talk about their feelings honestly.

- Both parties agree to acknowledge that their jobs are equally important.

- Both parties agree to speak every night, no matter what, even if only for five minutes.

Like a lot of guys with big egos, Will and Mike expected the other one to mind read and pick up slack in the relationship. They laughed over setting up a faux relationship contract, but were happier once they accepted how alike they were about work, and that they needed to check their egos at the door to communicate.

When you date, you spend a lot of time sizing up prospects. Imagine the shoe is on the other foot, and a potential date is sizing you up. How do you rate yourself? I don't mean to scare you off dating, though there are plenty of reasons to be afraid. After all, how many shrink couches are full of men on their backs unburdening dating horror stories?

If you plan on dating another man, you'll have to accept the very things in him that you have a hard time accepting in yourself.

17

THE M-WORD.
MADONNA?
MARRIAGE?
HELL, NO.
MONOGAMY!

Broaching the subject of monogamy in a gay male relationship is like baking a soufflé. Bake it for too short a period and it falls. Bake it too long and it dries up. The artful success of bringing up monogamy is in the timing. "Too much, too soon" is as bad as "too little, too late."

Forty-seven-year-old Scott, a travel agent from Florida, learned this lesson the hard way. After a great second date with thirty-seven-year-old Frank, when the attraction was heating up in the car ride back to Scott's place, Scott looked Frank in the eyes and said softly, "I really want to date you and only you from now on." In an awkward end to an otherwise fun evening, Frank suddenly remembered he had to be up early the next morning, exited the scene quickly, and never called Scott again. Scott now says he felt ridiculous after saying it and wishes he had blamed the outburst on a new and unusual strain of Tourette's syndrome called situational Tourette's. Though he didn't demand monogamy, the mere implication of the word so soon was enough to send Frank running. If Scott had veered the dinner conversation toward relationship history, the subject could have come up casually.

Forty-year-old musician Ted had the foresight to wait until the subject bubbled up to the surface naturally. After three months of dating Chris, a thirty-eight-year-old office manager in their hometown of New Orleans, the subject came up over drinks in the French Quarter. Chatting about the big gay party they were attending that evening, Chris said playfully, "If anyone comes on to you, I'll take him out. Some of these guys don't care if you are coupled off or not." Ted took the opportunity to ease into monogamy by offhandedly asking such questions as "What would happen if someone did ask you out? Would you date anyone else at this point?" and "What do you think about the two of us dating each other exclusively?" They agreed that they didn't want to date anyone else. And they were comfortable enough to say that if they ever felt like changing it in the future, they'd talk about it.

In addition to timing, there's another rule of thumb about monogamy in a gay male relationship. The guys who push monogamy—who demand it as a condition of dating and insist that it's the only way they can feel comfortable in a relationship with you—are always the first ones to cheat.

When my committed relationship with Karl ended after two and a half years, I started dating another man within weeks. The new guy, tall, blond, blue-eyed, thirty-six-year-old Doug, made it clear he didn't want to be "the rebound guy with someone newly broken up." He said it was absolutely necessary for us to be monogamous. I was flattered and wanted to show him I was serious, so I agreed (the road to hell is paved with flattery, not good intentions as some have claimed). Eleven months later, I discovered he had cheated, just once supposedly, while I was away on business. If he hadn't made such a big deal about our being monogamous, I doubt if this one incident would have been a deal breaker. After I pulled the "Sucker!" sticker off my back, I realized that my strong reaction to cheating was all about lying and the setup of this situation rather than the actual slip.

There is no getting around it—monogamy is what many gay men (and straight men, too, for that matter) say they want, but what few really want to give.

Let the subject of monogamy come up naturally once you have been together awhile. When it does, keep in mind these monogamy Mandates, which can help you establish a basis for discussion:

1. In the blush of infatuation, don't let your mouth write checks your ass can't cash.

Promising monogamy is flattering, makes you feel special,

and is *very* hard to go back on once you decide you don't want to practice it anymore.

2. Offer it unconditionally. If it's something you want soon into dating, consider offering it without demanding it back.

3. It's all about honest communication. If you decide that monogamy is something you both want, explore that if someone strays, the breakup issues are all about lies, betrayal, and a breakdown of honest communication. In my case, because we had set up monogamy as the rule, and because my guard was down, I felt blindsided. Since he had insisted on monogamy so strongly, it had never crossed my mind that he'd be the one to cheat.

4. Don't set the rule in stone. Agree that you will, as a couple, revisit the rules of your relationship if and when you choose.

 **HAVE THE FOLLOWING
SUDDENLY APPEARED IN
YOUR APARTMENT: AN
EXTRA TOOTBRUSH, A
SPARE CONTACT LENS
CASE, AND AT LEAST
TWO ARTICLES OF HIS CLOTHING?
CONGRATULATIONS! YOU HAVE A
BOYFRIEND**

Sometimes you can date a man for months and not know the status of your relationship. Is it love? Is it lust? Is it just a fling? As they say in Hollywood about films that stay in theaters a long time, "Does it have legs?"

Sometimes, by the middle of your first dinner, you are already planning your fifth-anniversary party.

Men being men, wanting what we want when we want it, it is hard to determine when you should clearly note the dating milestones. You know, the markers that indicate that your simple date has become a regular date and may well be on the road to real live boyfriend.

The following chart is a guide to help determine what category your man falls into, providing some key variables that will help you determine if he's a relationship trick or treat.

IS HE A RELATIONSHIP SHORT-TERM TRICK OR LONG-TERM TREAT?

WHAT CATEGORY IS HE?	WAYS YOU WILL BE ABLE TO TELL
TRICK	No last names.
	Minimal conversation. Probably e-mails rather than calls.
	Acts more transactional than an ATM machine.
	At least one drink but not one bite of food before or after sex.
UH,———(HIS NAME)	You just can't remember why you ever agreed to say more than hello to him, let alone why you ended up at dinner.
	During the middle of conversation, as he's telling you about his day at work, you can't remember what he does for a living.
	You find yourself flirting with your dinner waiter, whom you wouldn't normally glance at twice, just to keep yourself amused.

You have to remind yourself that it's rude not to look at him now and then as you're talking.

He's telling you about his last relationship and you're wondering what's on the *Frasier* rerun.

JUST A FRIEND

Makes a joke to others about the lack of attraction between the two of you.

You find you actually enjoy hearing about some date he had.

He refers to an ex repeatedly to demonstrate that he is clinging to some shred of this guy and, thus, is emotionally unavailable.

He tells you in detail of a recent STD, rash, or unusual physical malady.

UNSURE OF STATUS

You are more nervous than usual.

You talk generically about "friends" without naming or classifying anyone.

You ask each other ten times in one night if the movie one of you selected is okay.

WHAT CATEGORY IS HE?	WAYS YOU WILL BE ABLE TO TELL
	The word *okay* is used in more than five sentences a night (Is Shun Lee Palace okay for dinner? Is seven forty-five an okay time?).
POTENTIAL DATE FROM HELL	Shows up an hour late, and he's sniveling.
	Shows up wearing one of those slinky, silky, brightly colored suits and matching shoes with pointed toes from the International Male catalog.
	Cannot keep his eyes focused on anything, including you.
	Is he on crystal meth? Has he overdosed on coffee? You don't care.
	His eyes are on "cruise control" and his head swivels more than Linda Blair's in *The Exorcist*.
GOOD DATE	You laugh. With him, not silently at him as you do with your bad dates. Time flies by.
	You're listening to what he says, but your eyes keep landing on his mouth.

You make plans to get together for the movie you both want to see as you're talking about it, not later.

He gets more attractive as the evening wears on.

You both try to pick up the dinner check.

BOYFRIEND

Starts off a message on your answering machine by saying, "Hi, it's me."

Always has your numbers—phone, fax, cell phone, beeper—where you'll be staying if you travel.

You wait until he's in the other room before you play your telephone messages.

You wake up one morning and notice an extra toothbrush, electric shaver, baseball cap, and contact lens case—all under your bathroom sink.

MORE SERIOUS BOYFRIEND

Always has some sort of opinion about your evening, whether he was with you or not.

You give him access to your e-mail account.

Have the Following Suddenly Appeared in Your Apartment?

WHAT CATEGORY IS HE?	WAYS YOU WILL BE ABLE TO TELL
	Every decision you make from weekend plans to getting your haircut somehow involves his schedule.
	You suddenly realize you know every single appointment in his schedule book for the coming week, from his trip to the dentist to a lunch date with his sister.
FULL–BLOWN RELATIONSHIP	He has his own drawers in your bureau with several changes of clothes in your dresser and closet.
	He keeps a separate travel shaving kit in your hall closet along with other incidentals.
	You wouldn't mind if he made a weekend plan now and then without you, but you just haven't figured out a way to encourage it without coming across as uncaring about the relationship.
LOVER	Your mother talks to him first when she calls.
	The veterinarian asks to see both of you when Rover needs medical treatment.

	You look in your medicine cabinet and can't remember what toiletries are yours, and which are his.
	You share an answering machine.

Once you have assessed which category he falls under, adjust your behavior as a result. You obviously wouldn't treat him like a boyfriend if he was just a trick. You save that kind of attention for someone you know will want and earn it.

Don't make the mistake many do and put the cart before the horse. Don't rush a relationship, or you'll risk watching it crumble from the weight of too much pressure and too many expectations.

Do you remember that old Florence Henderson "Wessonality" TV commercial that included the line "Treat your family like company and your company like family"? That's great when you are entertaining friends and family, but it does not apply to dating. Don't treat your tricks like a lover, or your lover like a trick. Figure out what stage your relationship is in, and act accordingly.

19

AX THE WORD *EX*

Don't make the word *ex* the most important one in your vocabulary. Don't talk about more than two ex-lovers on any date, as in "Oh, my ex ate that way" or "My ex said the same damn thing about Barbra's new album."

Let's be honest here. In describing past relationships to someone new, you are either going to make yourself sound like the hapless victim (again!) of a dastardly dysfunctional man (how rare!) or, my usual choice, you'll end up sounding like the gay version of Heathcliff from *Wuthering Heights*—so noble, so loving, so pure.

How could all twenty-seven of those relationships have soured so, given your perfection? A family curse? A pox? Cruel fate? The plague? What Shakespeare called "ill conceit"? Just skip it, okay?

Playing the victim will get you the "pity look" and a nod of understanding and compassion that, believe me, will last as long as a snow cone in San Juan. You will never live up to the Heathcliff role, so step off the stage before your makeup runs in act 3.

As Shakespeare once said of romance gone wrong, "The course of true love never did run smooth." But that doesn't mean this should be the obsessive theme during a first date. Thirty-year-old Brent from Delaware, a self-described "romantic fool burned to a toasty crisp by my past three relationships," went to the movies and then dinner with good-natured Richard, also thirty. After mentioning for the tenth time that his "exes" treated him terribly, Brent came across like one of those lonesome losers on *Jerry Springer.* At dinner, Richard kept ordering margaritas in a futile attempt to literally drown all this pain, but Brent found an increasing number of ways to insinuate his dastardly exes into the conversation.

"Oh, yeah, my ex cheated on me, just like in that movie, but worse," he said. Richard listened silently (as if he could get a word in edgewise!) to sad ex stories and to tales of dates subsequent to the last ex that mysteriously hadn't flourished.

Three hours of ex stories later, they parted, and Brent drove home thinking Richard was physically attractive, a great listener, and someone he wanted to see again.

Richard drove home thinking Brent was physically attractive, way too in love with his own drama, and obviously damaged beyond repair.

Unless your last boyfriend's name really was Damien, don't waste time demonizing him to a stranger. You could be spilling your pain to a stranger, I should add, who might know your ex and have his own opinions given the small concentric circles of "gaydom."

You need to strike a balance of at least a little mystery and general acceptance of the past. Just indicate that it was bad timing, a great learning experience, irreconcilable differences, or that you have served your time for knocking him off and your parole officer says you don't have to discuss it anymore if you don't feel like it.

20

INTERGALACTIC INSTRUCTIONS ON CONQUERING CYBERSPACE

(Avoid the Darth Vaders Who Lurk in Chat Rooms and Find Your Own Luke Skywalker)

The term *lost in space* takes on a new meaning as thousands of men take to the Internet. Special gay Internet services like Gay.com and PlanetOut.com want to serve all of your gay needs, from travel to love to news. There are thousands of gay porn sites, and even *Business Week* acknowledged that the only two industries making any money on the Web are porn and ISPs. If you are in the mood to meet a man, AOL chat rooms offer rooms targeted to city and proclivity for every possible version of same-sex love. Chatting is a world of swapping GIFs and JPEGs, cyberpersonals, and endless possibilities. Conversation can range from numbingly banal to wrenchingly deep to wickedly naughty with each touch of the keyboard.

If straight people "surf" the Net, then gay men "cruise"

the Net. The options for meeting, chatting, and hooking up with other gay people are tremendous, with entirely new avenues of possibility for those who live in less populated areas, plus closet cases, fetishists, and married men. But the traffic is certainly not limited to those once-isolated groups. Deep in the heart of the most exciting city in the world, New York, the city that never sleeps, you'll discover some of the hottest men in the world holed up in their apartments trolling AOL's NYC m4m chat room.

Actress Sharon Stone, secretly a gay man trapped in a woman's body, once said, "Women might be able to fake orgasms. But men can fake whole relationships."

So how do you weed out the fakers from the real ones? How do you determine who is worth the time it'll take you to think up a clever screen name like Hotstud4love and who gets logged out of your life?

Here are some surefire do-and-don't guidelines for picking the winners and weeding out the losers:

DO AND DON'T GUIDELINES FOR ON-LINE DATING, WHEN YOU ARE LOOKING FOR MR. RIGHT AND NOT MR. RIGHT NOW		
	DO	DON'T
SCREEN NAME	Pick something simple, adventurous, and not too cutesy. Examples are	Warning: Whatever adjective you use in your screen name, you better

	DO	DON'T
SCREEN NAME	Adventurer2000 (descriptive), NYCgoodguy (narrows down location), or JPSprepman (initials and light description). These are infinitely better than something that makes you sound desperate (like Looking4lovenow or Mansearcher). Ask how many screen names he has—are you dealing with an on-line Sybil? AOL gives you up to seven per account. It is official Norman Bates–style psychosis if he has more than two.	be prepared to live up to it. Call yourself Funguy? You better be a million laughs when you meet, even after that bad day at work. Call yourself Horseman? Unless you are a jockey or a horse breeder, better not oversell the goods. And for God's sake, if you agree to meet some guy called Udo692me, don't expect flowers and candy.
WHERE TO MEET	Meet somewhere neutral but not sexless. Starbucks is sexless.	If you plan on seeing him twice, don't go to his house, and don't invite

Intergalactic Instructions on Conquering Cyberspace

DO AND DON'T GUIDELINES FOR ON-LINE DATING, WHEN YOU ARE LOOKING FOR MR. RIGHT AND NOT MR. RIGHT NOW

	DO	DON'T
WHERE TO MEET	That cool candlelit lounge downtown is not. Love cannot bloom when twenty-one-year-olds with tongue piercings are screaming out for lattes.	him to yours. Dial-up delivery sex is for one-nighters only. And don't meet him at a gay bar.
WHEN TO MEET	Agree to meet him if you still like him after you have spoken on the phone for a couple of weeks. You just need a little time to assess his consistency (you can always fake being nice to someone once).	Don't wait too long to meet. There's a fine line between not knowing enough, and building up too many expectations. You'll end up telling your entire life story to someone over weeks or months only to find upon meeting that he's more Phantom of the Opera than Sheikh of Araby, if you get my drift.
WHAT TO QUESTION	Question why he won't give you his	Ask as many questions as you can to weed out

	DO	DON'T
WHAT TO QUESTION	telephone number if you agree to meet. Is he married or too closeted? Question when the picture he sent was taken. If it's him posing by an Edsel wearing an "I Like Ike" button, move on.	losers, because people can mislead you on-line and via instant messages. But don't question his intentions too much. It's a blind date after all—despite the picture, the chatting, and eventually the hours on the phone pouring your heart out, please remember this—*you have never met him.* Hope for good chemistry but take the pressure off your first meeting.
PHONE NUMBER SWAP	Give him your home number if you decide you want to pursue a date. You need to	Don't give out your work number. Remember, Michael Douglas thought Glenn

Intergalactic Instructions on Conquering Cyberspace

DO AND DON'T GUIDELINES FOR ON-LINE DATING, WHEN YOU ARE LOOKING FOR MR. RIGHT AND NOT MR. RIGHT NOW		
	DO	**DON'T**
PHONE NUMBER SWAP	check him out for telephone chemistry.	Close was really sweet, too, when they first met in *Fatal Attraction*.

The most important advice for dating someone you meet in a chat room or from an on-line profile is this: no matter what his pictures look like, or what he's like in e-mails or on the phone, he'll probably be different in person, so keep your expectations in check. Internet introductions are the parallel universe of dating, completely contrary to what we're used to doing. Usually, if you meet a guy at a bar or a party, you act on whatever chemistry exists and later find out if you are compatible.

With on-line dating, you know all the details about his life and whether you share common interests and goals right away. You might even know intimate details because it's easy to reveal too much when you are creating a profile or a personal ad. Then you decide whether to meet him, at which point you find out if there's any chemistry.

Dating is all about compatibility and chemistry. With on-line dating, the order gets reversed. Your mind is a powerful tool and may wander off into dreamland quickly. Do everything you can to minimize your expectations. Hope for the best, be prepared for the worst, and set up the situation to your best advantage. Pick a meeting place where you're comfortable. Make light of the situation beforehand by letting him know that these things can be awkward and that you've found it's best to approach meeting as casually as possible.

21

RULE #1 FROM THE KENNEL APPLIES TO DATING: GIVE ROPE AND SPACE BUT NEVER LET THE DOG HAVE THE RUN OF THE YARD

●

Brad Davis. Profile: Hot-looking thirty-five-year-old. Decent, really tries to be a good man. Lawyer who made partner by thirty. Well-off. Nice family. Brad Davis. Single. Why?

Ask Brad Davis, a northern Californian now in his fourth year of therapy, why he's still single and he'll tell you. He's too independent. His relationships never last more than a few months. The defining breakup factor appears to be the same character traits his ex-boyfriends initially loved about Brad—namely, his independence and easygoing nature. After all, what's more attractive than a seemingly secure man who is comfortable within his own skin and undemanding?

Brad's mistake was not being independent and easygoing. His mistake was staying too easygoing after about three months of dating bliss.

After three months of a casual, laid-back approach to dating, decent, mellow Brad needed to access his inner hotheaded Latin lover and pitch a fit over something. A sideways glance from another man at his boyfriend. A bad day at work. The boyfriend's decision to spend an entire weekend with other friends. Most anything would have worked.

Of course, the immediate ramification will be a response like "What's wrong with you?" or "You are being unreasonable!" But this is when you have to remember that dating a gay man is not so different from raising a two-year-old. Gay men and two-year-olds test you. They want to know limits. Limits mean love. They want to know when they have been bad. They want to know that you are paying attention to them. They won't respect you if you always act whispery, levelheaded, and passive. In Brad's case, his boyfriends wound up doubting he cared because he was just too laid-back.

Of course the reason this approach will work for you, and not the hotheaded Latin lover, is this: you know when to quit.

Knowing when to quit will lead you to the best makeup sex you have ever had. But you can't wimp out and give in too soon. You have to know the fine line between maintaining an air of justified self-righteousness and holding on to a

Rule #1 from the Kennel Applies to Dating

111

grudge. You have to know the difference between being as-sertive and requiring a restraining order. But, as Brad is now learning, if you master this fine line for calculated ma-nipulation purposes only, you'll be able to control when and how you let go.

This isn't callous or cruel manipulation. This is being thoughtful and making your partner feel secure. Sometimes in the hope of establishing something long term with a boyfriend, guys mistakenly believe that being agreeable or malleable to all circumstances is attractive. It's not.

22

BE TRUE TO YOUR OWN STANDARDS

(And If You Don't Have Any, Get Some)

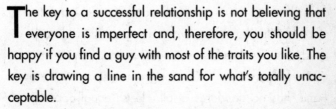

The key to a successful relationship is not believing that everyone is imperfect and, therefore, you should be happy if you find a guy with most of the traits you like. The key is drawing a line in the sand for what's totally unacceptable.

You have to decide what you absolutely cannot abide and then pray like hell you'll get over the rest. This is called having standards. Most people either have ridiculous standards or none at all.

When people meet thirty-five-year-old Steve, a banker in St. Louis, they wonder why he's single and why he'd have such trouble finding a decent date. He doesn't get it, either. "I am an attractive guy and a good catch," says not-so-modest Steve. "All I want is a good-looking, smart man who will sweep me off my feet." Sounds reasonable right? Who doesn't want that?

After some prodding about the type of guy Steve dates, the truth comes out. He is only interested in compulsive circuit-party boys and exhibitionist bodybuilders with less than 5 percent body fat who want to spend quiet weekends alone with him. He wants a guy that Mom would approve of, but Steve isn't out to his family so it's not like Mom is going to meet anyone. The only guy he'll date is someone wealthy but not snobby, popular but without too many friends who'll be a distraction, successful in his career but not too driven, and really comfortable being gay but, as Steve puts it, "no rainbow-wearing, drum-banging parade marcher." You get the picture. Steve has set up impossible standards for his dates. Why not add "Must be able to swim the English Channel" to the already overpopulated list of impossible standards?

Thirty-four-year-old Gordon from Boston, on the other hand, has no standards at all. He is "equal opportunity" when it comes to dating, and it gets him nowhere. He has more dates than anyone else I have ever seen, but they are all exercises in futility. Gordon's date-screening criterion is "Hello." If they say that, they are on the list. He is reasonably attractive and engaging but has no idea what he really wants out of dating, and that has led to deathly quiet dinners as he finds out midway through the second course that his date has nothing in common with him or was recently profiled on *America's Most Wanted*.

An ounce of prevention is worth a pound of cure. And before a date, a few minutes of well-thought-out screener questions about your lives and common interests can save a lot of wasted time later.

That's why you have to have your standards. Write them down, laminate them, and put them in your wallet. Why? Because the world at large, aided by alcohol, societal pressures, and the lateness of the hour at the bar or party, will conspire to make you settle.

Focus on the standards that matter to you, and make sure they are reasonable and attainable. Ask yourself if you would be able to achieve all the standards you set for one of your dates.

Here's a partial list of characteristics for you to mix and match and create your own list of standards:

- Has a paying job or other means of self-support
- Wants one-on-one intimacy leading to a long-term relationship
- Spiritual, believes in a higher power, that there's a plan
- Drinks socially
- Drinks constantly
- Does drugs now and then
- Drug dealers call him when they are low on cash
- Very social, actually believes you can be close, intimate friends with hundreds of gay men if you throw enough parties

Be True to Your Own Standards

- Likes the outdoors, into hiking and being outside
- Likes the two seconds he is outside while racing to his heated or air-conditioned car
- Similar sex drive
- No outstanding warrants for his arrest
- No outstanding warrants for his arrest in your state
- Wants to have children
- Will consider having children
- Doesn't want children because he is one
- Has compatible sexual appetite and proclivities
- Is HIV-negative or HIV-positive, depending on your status and feelings about that
- Believes in monogamy
- Believes in "if it moves, jump on it"
- Within four inches either way of your height
- Height and weight proportionate
- Has an extraordinary _____ (for fetishists, pick your body part)
- Has been in a faithful, long-term (over a year) relationship before
- Has the same relative degree of "outness" that you do
- Socially acceptable manners
- When he eats, talks with his mouth completely full

23

DON'T TRY TO BE OZZIE AND HARRIET— EVEN OZZIE AND HARRIET WEREN'T OZZIE AND HARRIET

(And They Were Straight)

●

Gay men make a huge mistake when they choose to act like the perfect 1950s straight couple so that they'll fit into some ancient definition of American success.

Ozzie and Harriet, the quintessential symbols of post–World War II American domestic bliss, had their share of problems that the world never saw, and you will, too. Be more like the other Ozzy (as in Osbourne) and let it all hang out.

Living twenty-four hours a day with an internalized ideal of how love should be is exhausting for anyone. But it's a tougher road for gay people, and few walk that road without at least one fairly large carry-on bag full of relationship issues. For instance, how do you create a relationship with so few gay role models? How open or closeted are you as a couple? Do you feel shame about your relationship? Do friends and family know about you? Do the people at work think you are just roommates? Do both sides of your families treat you with respect as a couple, just as they do your straight siblings?

Chances are you will have to endure more than most straight people when it comes to merging two gay lives. The best way to manage that is to reset the expectation of how easy coupling with another man will be.

As you navigate the ups and downs of a new relationship, just remember that you:

1. Don't have to adopt dating or relationship roles (he cooks, you clean) just because your parents did.

2. Can have more freedom in your daily lives if you choose. Men like freedom, and you don't need to adapt to some straight norm that makes no sense for you. You can be more flexible with your schedules, more open about what you do together and apart than the traditional straight-couple norm.

3. Do need to demand equal rights. For instance, your partner should be treated the same as your siblings' spouses. Your parents and family may have come so far as to be accepting of your partner, but still not include him in family events, pictures, etc. Demand that treatment is fair and equal for him.

4. Should build a strong foundation of communication with your partner about your coupling experiences. Are people treating you differently from when you were single? Is it hard at times to see yourself as part of a couple? What do you like and not like about the structure you are creating for your relationship?

24

BE YOUR OWN "JUDGE JUDY" WITH RELATIONSHIP MISTAKES: EVALUATING HEINOUS VS. FORGIVABLE SINS

Your boyfriend goes out late with his pals and doesn't get in until 2 A.M. He has had some laughs, a few drinks, and now, sheepishly, he sneaks into your room hoping that you forgot he said he'd be home by 11 P.M. You didn't forget. In fact, you sit up, turn on the light, and all of a sudden you've been transformed from a tall, preppy-looking man who wears contacts into a short Jewish woman with your own TV show and spectacles lodged at the edge of your nose. You have become Judge Judy, and now he is on trial for having screwed up.

So what's forgivable within a relationship and what isn't?

Certainly a night out with pals that gets a little carried

away can be forgiven—with flowers or perhaps a subtle deposit into your mutual fund account. But how do you distinguish what's forgivable from the "deal breaker," that one act that, justifiably, should put you over the edge?

The following chart explains how to evaluate forgivable sins versus deal breakers:

THE CATALOG OF SINS	FORGIVABLE	DEAL BREAKER
Lying	Doesn't tell you how many men he has slept with in his life. Instead you get a little white lie—"Oh, just six or seven, honey."	You are living together in your new jointly owned house and you find out he owes $200,000 (not counting penalties) in back taxes to the IRS.
Cheating	You officially break up after you hit that six-month "make or break" moment, and you find out after you have recommitted as a couple that	He's the one who insisted on monogamy, which you agreed to, and you discover that his definition of monogamy means "free sex

THE CATALOG OF SINS	FORGIVABLE	DEAL BREAKER
	your boyfriend slept with someone during your "break."	anywhere but your house."
Breaking a date	He calls in advance, apologizes profusely, and insists on having a "reschedule date" set right away so he can make it up to you.	He sends a cancellation e-mail to you within a few hours of your date, with no explanation, never calls to follow up, and doesn't set up an alternative plan.
Sins of omission	He forgets your birthday but makes it up to you with a really great dinner and gift.	He forgets your birthday completely. Even after you tell him, he shrugs it off as no big deal.

THE CATALOG OF SINS	FORGIVABLE	DEAL BREAKER
Sins of commission	After a party with your friends, you're walking home and he gets mad and unreasonable and starts demanding to know where your relationship is going.	You're actually *at* the party with your friends, and he gets mad and unreasonable and, in front of everyone, starts demanding to know where your relationship is going.
Social acknowledgment	You have been dating almost a year, the L-word has been uttered, and you are planning trips as a couple. You meet him at a party where he is talking with new people, and he introduces you as his "friend."	You have been dating almost a year, the L-word has been uttered, and you are planning trips as a couple. You meet him at a party where he is talking with new people, and he turns to you as you walk up and says, "And you are . . . ?"

25

THE FINAL MANDATE—INTEGRATE, INTEGRATE BEFORE IT'S TOO LATE!

●

If you are serious about coupling, it's important to make a public statement at an appropriate time in your relationship. Unfortunately, the two huge issues here rarely seem to go hand in hand. The first issue is "public statement." The second is "appropriate time."

A public statement is pretty clear: it can range from a simple "friends and family" announcement to moving in together. You are letting the world know you are a couple.

The appropriate time, on the other hand, is not clear. When is the right time to commit publicly? Many gay men I spoke with seem to delay making an announcement as long as possible.

The drive to hibernate with a new love, to stay in and eat Papa John's delivered pizza for six months, might be stronger among gay people because they can avoid a double dose of trouble: public scrutiny from straight people, and even worse scrutiny from gay people. But this scrutiny is all part of integrating.

With straight friends, any new partner for their gay pal is a big deal, especially if you are their household's token homosexual. They are probably more anxious than you are to see their spirited gay friend settle down. Their image of the "gay lifestyle," the same image you grew up with, has you running around far too much with all sorts of bizarre characters and doing back flips in bathhouses. It follows that when you bring someone reasonable into their midst, you'll look on with horror as they descend on the poor soul, hoping to push "you two crazy kids" one step closer to a white house and picket fence. This is the kind of social pressure that childless straight Mormon couples complain about.

But that's still easier than dealing with the gay guys. When you think of introducing a new boyfriend, do you recoil at the pressure you face walking into a party of precocious queens with too much time on their hands? Do you flinch at the thought of their checking you out head to toe, sizing you up as if you were two stylish cows walking into McDonald's? Do you think straight couples face this pressure quite as much?

That's the downside of integrating, but there's a worse downside to hibernating. Though you will be blissfully happy on your island, eventually you have to leave the island and wash ashore to your real lives, filled with friends

and family. I am convinced that this coming ashore is when many gay couples hit the skids. You underestimate the pressure you'll feel when merging your lives.

Many of us have been living an extended bachelor's existence when we finally meet the guy we want as our partner. We aren't used to having anyone question our financial situation (bank accounts, bills, investments), witness our family dynamics, listen to our telephone answering machine messages, see our mail and/or e-mail, or know our daily patterns.

Usually, this period of learning the details of each other's life is where privacy fears and compatibility issues arise, and where compromises have to occur.

George and Ron, two forty-something corporate executives in Wisconsin trying to build a life together, thought they were a perfect fit in every way until they started spending seven nights a week together. George, an early bird, was staying up much later than usual to spend time with Ron, a night owl. By the time Ron got home from work and the gym and started fixing dinner, it was 9 P.M. and George was ready for bed. This discrepancy wasn't an issue until they lived together. When they were dating, they overlooked their time differences and wrote off a little sleep deprivation. But soon they could no longer dismiss the negative impact of George's "up with the roosters" mornings or Ron's "midnight moon" evenings on their limited time together. They decided to compromise and devised a gay version of daylight saving time: George set his internal clock ahead one hour, and Ron set his back by an hour, netting them two hours together a day.

It sounds simplistic, but compatibility when it comes to basics like sleep is key. One of the upsides to integrating relatively soon is that you'll learn his habits. You'll find out how he feels about sharing important issues like money. And you'll find out right away that his family hates you, so you'll save a ton on wasted holiday gifts, phone calls, and other vain attempts to win them over. You made their son gay. That he knew every Bette Midler song by the time he was twelve is beside the point. Once you start dating him, it's all about you.

Talking to gay guys about relationships, I heard many stories of fiery flames that fizzled into dying embers at the point of integration. We all agreed that if we could do one thing differently in past relationships, we would have followed this final mandate. Integrate sooner, and shorten that wonderful and lulling cocooning honeymoon if you are entertaining thoughts of longer-term love.

The truth is that I have cocooned more than a jar of caterpillars. And I enjoyed every minute of it, too. But after cartons of Chinese food delivered in, lots of movies on the VCR, and long nights in front of the fireplace getting to know each other, a quicker way to assess longer-term dating and relationship potential would have been to invite friends over for dinner after about month two.

You will know by then if he is worth the introductions and ensuing expectations that'll descend on the two of you.

Once you introduce him, he becomes a staple of your conversations, as in "How's Michael?"—until you inform them Michael is no longer in the picture.

Before you invest too much time in a man, see how he treats your friends and family. If he really cares about you, he will make an effort to join your life, already in progress. Social interaction is also a surefire way for you to find out more about each other, and how you fit in the world together as a couple.

Had I done this, I would have spared myself the difficulties of disentangling after months of dating because the seemingly great guy I had picked was unsuited to me, closeted, or totally uninterested in being what I now call a "boyfriend outside the home."

In Part I, you discovered how the twenty-five Mandates work. Part II focuses on gay dating behaviors. What works? What doesn't? And what are the lines you should avoid at all costs? Call it Gay Dating 101.

Truthfully, there's a lot to remember on a date. Chew with your mouth closed. Occasionally stop talking about yourself long enough to ask a perfunctory question. Act like an urban Narcissus and check out how you look in every window, mirror, and reflecting surface you pass. Stand up straight (it might be the only straight thing you do all night).

That's why, when it comes to dating activities, the dos and don'ts need to be clearly spelled out.

PART II

A Gay Dating Primer: Dos and Don'ts

DATING DOS AND DON'TS

●

W hen it comes to dating, from calling him for that first date to meeting his friends and family, clear dos and don'ts are associated with each activity.

DATING ACTIVITY	DOS	DON'TS
Calling him for the first date	Keep it relatively short (five minutes).	Drone on and on about your life.
The first telephone conversation	Keep it light.	Get his opinion on your conflict with the guy in your office whom you hate.
Watching your first video together	Light, funny comedies like *My Best Friend's Wedding* or *As Good As It Gets.*	AIDS dramas, war movies, westerns, and bitchy girl-friend dramas like *Beaches* and *The Women,* unless you want another sister.

DATING ACTIVITY	DOS	DON'TS
Going somewhere great for dinner	Make a reservation at an out-of-the-way, quiet spot with candles and a romantic ambience.	Go to your version of Cheers, where "everyone knows your name," unless Zagat's also knows their name.
Meeting his friends for the first time	Take the lead and set up dinner at a neutral spot with no more than two of them, preferably a committed couple.	Wait until the "beach house" birthday party or some other event where his closest "pack" will be together, celebrating some regular event in their lives, just waiting for you, newcomer.
Speaking to his mom on the phone	Just listen, and say nice things about her kids.	Bitch about your own family, tell her how you hate your father, and ignore her pleas for you to get counseling.

A Gay Dating Primer: Dos and Don'ts

DATING ACTIVITY	DOS	DON'TS
Having dinner with his parents	Pick a quiet spot with decent value, basic food, and valet parking. The key word is *seamless*—have a seamless evening with a steady, pleasant pace.	Go to Rock 'n' Roll Sushi, the cool new sushi and sashimi restaurant bar that has no convenient parking but features an open-mike for local bands during dinner.
Sex on the first date	Don't, unless you are in a foreign country, and one of you is leaving the next day.	Don't, unless you are in a foreign country, and one of you is leaving the next day.
Running into coworkers when you're on a date	Stop, introduce your date by his name, and see if you can set a world record for how quickly you can mention the odd coincidence of running into one other along with best wishes for a fun evening.	Panic, act nervous, and try to divert him, as if police dogs have picked up the scent of the drugs you swallowed before leaving Bogotá. He'll think you are ashamed of him or a complete closet case.

DATING ACTIVITY	DOS	DON'TS
Sex dates	Make it clear that, even though this may become a regular thing, this is not something you'll be adding to your Palm Pilot.	Forget that even though they sometimes seem like real dates, they aren't.
Drinking and drugging	If you do drink and drug more than socially and want someone who also does this, you might want to refer to yourself as a "party boy" several times during the evening. The proclivities of a thirty-five-year-old man who calls himself a party boy are clearer than Morse code.	If you drink and drug occasionally and *don't* want to bring this to the forefront of his consciousness as he sizes you up as husband material, don't mention the recent suture of your deviated septum, or that there's nothing like Special K to start off your morning, especially after a night of ecstasy.

A Gay Dating Primer: Dos and Don'ts

DATING ACTIVITY	DOS	DON'TS
Buying condoms	Approach this confidently; after all, using condoms shows respect for yourself and your partner. This is a valuable quality to have, you should be proud of it.	Dress in disguise with a baseball cap lowered to cover your face, fidget in the cash register line, and buy a wide variety of household and personal items you don't really need hoping the clerk won't notice the twenty-pack of ribbed, nonlubricated rubbers.
Leaving a message on his machine	Make it brief, amusing, and purposeful, as in "Thanks for a great evening" or "Are you free on the twelfth?"	Approach leaving a message on his machine with all the self-absorption of your therapy session, with lots of indecisive *ums*, breathy pauses, and too much information.

DATING ACTIVITY	DOS	DON'TS
Running into your ex-lover on one of your first dates with a new guy	Nod an acknowledgment from afar if you are friendly, or steadfastly avoid his gaze if you are not. If he approaches the two of you, a quick hello as if greeting an old acquaintance is all that's needed. Quickly adapt to your circumstances and realize that you are late for the film you are seeing or are in dire need of another drink at the party, or quickly devise a similar polite yet immediate exit strategy.	Beam at the ex and be overly friendly, grabbing his arm and saying to your date, *"This* is the Frank I have been telling you about," *or better yet,* avoid him in a dramatic way, ending your evening with plaintive sobs about how you thought you were over it, but running into Frank is something you "really have to process."

135

DATING ACTIVITY	DOS	DON'TS
Evaluating "life mate" potential	Wait until you have experienced him for at least two seasons of the year before you even start to evaluate his long-term potential. How a gay man acts during each of the seasons is telling. The summer personality can be very different from the winter one.	Start planning your home together even if you have great chemistry and are comfortable with each other after a few weeks. You need to experience each other's daily schedules, routines, and core beliefs in action before you can evaluate long-term potential.

PICKUP LINES GUARANTEED TO FAIL:
A DEFINITE DATING DON'T!

●

Finally, here is a sampling of pickup lines that have been used for years and known to fail every time.

DON'T USE THEM.
DON'T DATE ANYONE WHO DOES.

1. Quick, give me an M&M—you make me go into sugar shock.

2. I wouldn't normally do this kind of thing.

3. You look just like that porno star what's his name.

4. Can I borrow a quarter? I promised I'd call my mother as soon as I fell in love.

5. Are you tired from running through my mind?

6. How about a Scotch and sofa?

7. (Grab his collar, look at the inside, and say) Sorry, I thought it said "Made in Heaven."

8. I lost my number. Can I have yours?

9. How about breakfast? Shall I call you or nudge you?

10. Has anyone ever told you that you look like the future?

11. You complete me. (Said with trembling voice, à la Jerry Maguire)

12. You know, I couldn't pull off wearing clothes like that but somehow you can.

13. I was thinking of going back to being straight, but with a butt like yours, we should talk.

14. Get out of my dreams. Get into my Chevette.

15. I'm writing a book on dating. May I ask you a few questions?

PART III

The Who, What, Where, and How of Meeting a Guy

I t's all about editing," a wise old queen named David told me recently, with all the haute grandeur of that real wise old queen Elizabeth II. David, seventy-three years young, was commenting on the state of gay dating these days, compared to when he was in his thirties. "It's easier and it's harder," he said. "Easier, because you can be more open and there are more options for meeting and more support for building a healthy relationship. Harder, because there are too many options for single gay men nowadays. How does a poor gay guy keep it all straight?"

Do matchmakers work? Does whom you meet a man through make any difference to your dating experience? What types of gay guys are out there and what can you expect from each? Where are the best and worst places to meet? In the Internet age, on-line dating can be awkward at times, but it's rapidly become one of the most viable ways for busy single gay guys to meet and date. How do you develop a winning profile, along with strategies for making the most of your on-line dates?

WHOM YOU MEET HIM THROUGH

Part of the "meeting" equation is, of course, evaluating his potential based on who introduced the two of you or set you up, if it's a blind date. The following chart rates his potential success or failure as a mate taking into account how much credibility your matchmaker has.

WHOM TO TRUST AS A REFERENCE	RATING THEIR JUDGMENT, FROM ! = AWFUL! TO !!!!! = AWESOME!
MOTHER	! He is probably more asexual than an amoeba. The best way out of this date without being rude to someone your mother picked is to carry a small bottle of ipecac (the treatment for poisoning—it makes you puke on cue) and use it the first chance you get as your escape.
SISTER	!! He is probably a nice guy but not your type at all. Just think about it. Your *sister* wants a guy for you, *like you*, or more like it, as *she* perceives you. This is dangerous at best.
FATHER (LONG SHOT; BUT COULD HAPPEN. WITNESS THE	!!!! Your dad wouldn't fix you up with a dork. He understands the shallow aspects of dating probably all too well from his youth.

WHOM TO TRUST AS A REFERENCE	RATING THEIR JUDGMENT, FROM ! = AWFUL! TO !!!!! = AWESOME!
FILM *THE SUM OF US*)	This will help counteract his homophobia.
FRIENDS	!!! A true friend will know you, and even if the chemistry is off, at least the guy will be plausible. Otherwise, get new friends.
COMPETITIVE FRIENDS	–! He will bark like a dog when he appears at your door. Be sure to take a can of Off! with you when you head out for "disaster date"—that is, unless you find yourself suddenly, inexplicably ill moments after you greet him and apologize as you take to your bed. Note: Everyone has one or two pals one could call competitive, whom we keep around for amusement sake, if nothing else. Key to making these pseudofriendships work is your taste for vengeance. Remind your "competitive friend" that paybacks are a bitch, and so are you.

WHOM TO TRUST AS A REFERENCE	RATING THEIR JUDGMENT, FROM ! = AWFUL! TO !!!!! = AWESOME!
NEIGHBORS	!½ He will be interested in classical music you've never heard of and food you can't pronounce. You will stare at each other blankly over your wine until the check arrives, wondering what you ever did to your neighbor that she would be so cruel in return.
COWORKER	!!!! He will be charming. Coworkers know they have to face you every single day for at least eight hours. They won't gamble as much with a vested interest.
THAT NICE OLD LADY FROM CHURCH	!!! A hit-or-miss proposition, but he might actually be okay. She is not as clueless as you might think. She's seen a lot in her years, and she is sick of being underestimated as that "little old lady." She probably rocked in her day with a few hotties no one knew about.

WHOM TO TRUST AS A REFERENCE	RATING THEIR JUDGMENT, FROM ! = AWFUL! TO !!!!! = AWESOME!
THE GYM FLOOR ATTENDANTS	!!! A decent rating only because of the likelihood of his good body. In the extremely rare instance of a trainer who actually picked someone for you based on his mind, there could be a conflict. But you are safe in assuming that your gym trainer will be looking out for the shallow side of you, as he would for him. Note: There are many ways to date an attractive-looking sexual compulsive with loser tendencies. But this is the quickest. Be aware that after you go out with him once, everyone at your gym will know and you will start receiving knowing looks and secret handshakes as if you had joined some secret club. Guess what? You did.
THE INTERNET	!! A total gamble based on whether the chemistry will work, but at least you can know a little more about him and his life before spending

WHOM TO TRUST AS A REFERENCE	RATING THEIR JUDGMENT, FROM ! = AWFUL! TO !!!!! = AWESOME!
	face time with him. And if there's chemistry, you get to move ahead a little more quickly.
MEETING HIM ON YOUR OWN	!!!!! Sadly, this is still the most surefire way to know if he's right for you. As the Mandates attest, you can quickly assess whether he's right for you.

WHAT TYPES ARE OUT THERE? FROM "BOY NEXT DOOR" TO "BILLY THE GAY CLONE" DOLL–TYPE YOUR HEART OUT AND FIND OUT WHICH TYPE HE IS

I know, I know. You hate to stereotype—but do it anyway because it's on target more often than not!

All right, everyone clasp your hands together, breathe deeply, and tell yourself that we are all unique beings under the sun. Sit in the lotus position with thumb to forefingers in an upward circle and breathe in light. This is perfectly fine for yoga class, or even for that visit to the Buddhist center. But, walk down any street with a sizable gay male population and give me a dollar for each of the following you see:

• San Francisco plaid shirt/bandanna–wearing clone with close-cropped hair and a Gauguin beard

• Beefed-up, flat-topped, jeans, white T-shirt, and black boot–wearing Chelsea boy

• Khaki-wearing, slightly-older-than-he-looks guppie

• Diesel jeans–wearing, Prada-shoed, sleek-haired glamour man

• Abercrombie & Fitch sweatshirt–wearing, tousled-on-purpose jock-still-in-college wanna-be

Okay, it might not be everyone, but I'd still have enough money for dinner.

Each gay type comes with its own set of personality traits. Is it unfair to judge a book by its cover? Of course, it is. Are you sometimes mistaken? Yes. Is it worth the risk to do it anyway? Absolutely. Las Vegas odds are with you.

So belly up to the betting table and put your money on the table to ready you for what you are getting yourself into. Which of the following is he?

BOY NEXT DOOR	He's sweet and wants a boyfriend desperately, but possibly for the wrong reasons, such as "gay social acceptance." Often idealizes love, which makes it hard for you to be as real with each other as a healthy relationship requires.
LEATHER QUEEN	You will always be second-fiddle mistress to the fetish. As you stare into each other's eyes during an evening out, be prepared for a lightninglike shift of focus as some "Mary" in a dog halter saunters by.
ARTIST	You'll love his self-absorption and his dedication to his work. That is, you'll love it from afar. It's more attractive from afar.
BILLY THE GAY CLONE DOLL	What are all the other gay guys doing? They are? Well, date him and guess what. You will, too!
TWELVE-STEPPER	Be prepared to listen, and listen, and listen. After three months, you'll be able to take his place and recite his

qualification when he has to miss leading his AA meeting. His upside is self-awareness and penchant for growth. The downside is the constant questioning of others' motives, habits, and relative sanity.

CITY KID

He grew up riding the subway, talking with people . . . and he now needs to talk to people constantly. Try, just try being alone with him for more than a day. It's not a matter of *if,* it's a matter of *when* you will go nuts.

PREPSTER

The old boy network and ideals are alive and well. The new millennium's version is more self-aware and socially conscious, but you have to live with the ongoing jokester sense of humor and a fashion sense that stops with khakis.

PROFESSIONAL MAN

He's looking for either a successful, well-off mirror image, or he has a weakness for inappropriate, probably younger, men.

BOHEMIAN	You'll be charmed by his willingness to thumb up his nose at convention, but when push comes to shove, and you try to integrate him into your life of family and friends, look out.
OTHERWISE STRAIGHT	Incredibly charming, the kind of guy you wanted since you were in college, which is mentally where he still is—trying to figure himself out, not willing to accept being gay. The good part is that he doesn't have all the gay baggage—too many late nights, too many boyfriends, a willingness to suffer fools just a little too gladly in the name of being a gay social gadfly—but has plenty of closet baggage. He can't decide if he's gay, is terrified anyone will suspect, and you'll always wonder if—given the choice of you or lying—he'd pick you.
BI-CURIOUS	Uses terms like *straight acting and appearing* as if no one knows he is a big queen. Guards his denial like the crown jewels.

Of course, typing doesn't always work. There is the re- mote chance you'll be surprised when the boy next door turns out to be next door to a sex club.

Once, my clean-cut friend Steven visited a well-known bar in San Francisco. He reported back to me, "Amidst the bears, the leather queens, and the assorted diesel dykes stood this one cute, 'preppyish' guy who definitely didn't belong in the setting. Feeling that I had found a kindred soul, I approached him, said hello, and struck up a conver- sation.

"Sensing a mutual attraction, I blurted out that I'd much rather the two of us were in a nice, quiet restaurant where we could enjoy each other's company in peace. It was then that he shared with me that we would have an opportunity to go out: he had a club meeting to which he would like to invite me. He pulled out a card and scribbled his name and phone number on the back as I inquired about the club. He told me to read the card. There it was: 'Sigma . . . the club for sadists and masochists.'

"I decided not to find out which one he was . . . or whether I was either."

WHERE YOU MEET HIM

The good and bad news is that nowadays you can meet a potential date anywhere. Thank God we no longer live in the kind of restrictive society where suitable mates originate only from social introductions and the best schools in New England. That's a good thing.

But the variety of options for meeting potential dates and mates can be confusing. Just remember that the twenty-five Mandates always apply and can help you navigate successfully through the maze of expanded high-tech options.

Here are tips and strategies for maximizing your chances of a successful dating experience, when you meet him in any of the following places or situations:

PLACES WHERE YOU CAN MEET HIM	TIPS FOR MAKING THE PLACE HEAVEN INSTEAD OF HELL
ON–LINE THROUGH A CHAT ROOM (SEE THE TOP TEN TIPS FOR ON–LINE DATING, ON PP. 161–164)	Wake up and smell the coffee, Little Red Riding Hood. People lie. He'll tell you he's six foot three, 190 pounds, and blue eyed, yet when you arrive at the designated bar to meet him, he is 250 pounds if he's an ounce. Get a picture first and meet in a neutral place for a drink, so you can make a quick getaway. Inviting him to your house, or going to his, is a surefire way to ensure you won't end up dating. Don't write anything in an IM that you wouldn't say to his face when he is, hopefully,

The Who, What, Where, and How of Meeting a Guy

151

PLACES WHERE YOU CAN MEET HIM	TIPS FOR MAKING THE PLACE HEAVEN INSTEAD OF HELL
	sitting across from you on a real date.
	And as a friend of mine says, "Avoid the boys who live on-line."
STRAIGHT BARS	You are out on the town with friends from work, and you spot him across the room, also with a group of straight friends. It is a little awkward, maybe even dangerous, to try to meet him on your own. That's when you deploy the "We are going to hook you up with one of the 'hottie' women from that mixed group over there" to your unsuspecting single, straight male colleague. Your benevolence will pay off when the two groups start to mix, and you'll be introduced to the guy you like in a seamless way.
LOW–KEY GAY BARS	Stand near the bar. It's the most obvious place if you want to meet someone.
	Play pool. You can always say that you are not a barfly, but it's so hard

to find a good billiards table that you come to the Roundup every week to get a couple of games in.

HIGH–MAINTENANCE GAY BARS

Ignore him but not in a mean way, yet stay in his line of sight. It worked for Lana Turner at Schwab's. And you believed all those stories of her being "discovered"?

BARS THAT SERVE FOOD (ALSO KNOWN AS GAY RESTAURANTS)

Buy him a drink and have the waiter take it to him at his table.

RESTAURANTS

You spot him as you are perusing the menu. Do not order anything that requires more than three utensils or a bib to eat. You need light food, food that will allow you to flirt. Get the grilled tuna. It's light, it's bite-size, you can eat it without looking like a slob as you slowly stare a wall through him.

PLACES WHERE YOU CAN MEET HIM	TIPS FOR MAKING THE PLACE HEAVEN INSTEAD OF HELL
GLITZY DANCE PALACES	Go with a group of friends, as a major club like The Roxy is no place to go alone. When you spot him, smile and give him that look that says, "I am trapped with these people—save me." Keep smiling as you are talking with your friends, and glance over at him every minute or so.
DOWN–AND– DIRTY GAY "ESTABLISH– MENTS"	Your goal in going to a leather bar like New York's The Lure probably wasn't to meet the man you'd marry. More like it, you went to meet the man voted Most Likely to Own a Sling by the Time He's 20 in high school. Nonetheless, there he is, someone who makes you want to buy the ring and rent the church. It doesn't even bother you that he's wearing more leather than the entire cast of a Roy Rogers/Dale Evans movie. The solution is to (a) stop visualizing him slung up on a hook like he's a piece of cattle, and (b)

	talk to him about anything other than where you are—college, where he lives, movies—to see if he's a hard-core fetishist (in which case he'll skulk away) or a decent guy out experimenting a little.
CHURCH	Don't sing each hymn as if you were Ethel Merman trying to get noticed. Remember to give at least $5 to the collection plate. The last thing you want him doing is ruling you out as a potential bad tipper.
900 #S	Though it will be hard to tell people at your wedding that you "met" at 1–900–HOT–BODS, I have known couples that met this way. Despite their intention when calling, they refrained from any telephone activity and ended up making plans for dinner at another time.
DATING SERVICES	They can cost a lot of money and usually they seem to be run by

155

PLACES WHERE YOU CAN MEET HIM	TIPS FOR MAKING THE PLACE HEAVEN INSTEAD OF HELL
	people who have more chance of winning the lottery than having a successful dating relationship themselves.
TWELVE–STEP PROGRAMS	Do you or does anyone in your family, immediate or otherwise, exhibit any of the following behaviors: alcoholism, drug addiction, overeating, and/or sexual compulsivity? If so, run, don't walk, to the nearest gay Al Anon (or other twelve-step support group) meeting, where you will find a roomful of gay guys who at least have the self-awareness to identify issues and problems, a requisite skill for relationships.
PARTIES	Don't wait for someone to come up to you. Hopefully, you are at a party of friends and not the gay equivalent of a "kegger," a house party of strangers, so that the crowd will be semicontrolled high quality.

PLACES WHERE YOU CAN MEET HIM	TIPS FOR MAKING THE PLACE HEAVEN INSTEAD OF HELL
"DATE BAIT" PARTIES: THE NEW TREND OF ORGANIZING GAY SINGLES PARTIES BY INCLUDING ON–THE–SPOT COMPUTER MATCHUPS	Standing up in a crowd of gay male strangers and, in one minute, telling them why you are datable, and what you want in a man, will make a man of even the toughest marine. Can you think of anything ballsier, especially if you stand up confidently and with a wry sense of humor about it all? Perhaps it will even get you a date with one of the marines in the room the night you attend your first "date bait" party.
SPEED DATING	Speed dating sounds a little "Wham, grrr, thank you, sir," doesn't it? It can seem like that with stopwatches, folding chairs, and name tags instead of candles and good music. Having to stick to first names and not reveal contact information like phone numbers makes you want to just blurt them out. But it's not so bad if you avoid acting like you're on a job interview. Despite the time constraints of cramming everything you can into

PLACES WHERE YOU CAN MEET HIM	TIPS FOR MAKING THE PLACE HEAVEN INSTEAD OF HELL
	seven-minute intervals with a rotating crop of strangers in an ambience best described as "antiromance," keep your sense of humor. Of course, it's an awkward way to meet. But it's also efficient, so you don't need to feel like a pathetic loser. Most guys have spent two hours of their time on far more worthless dating pursuits such as barhopping. Corral a friend into going with you. That way, you have someone to make sly eye contact with, to break the tension and ease your nerves. Unlike date bait, at least speed dating is about one-to-one connection. You don't have to stand before an entire room with one pressurized shot to make your case.
GYM	Be friendly but not fawning. Chances are you go to the gym regularly, so unless you want to be thought of as "Chatty Cathy," limit your stares and awkward intros to the ones who really count. The worst part about

	meeting someone at the gym is breaking through the crowd if his gay posse surrounds him, or if he works out with a partner. It's harder to break the ice. But don't let loitering gym queens with their asses velcroed together keep you from your guy. Maintain eye contact and think of something intelligent to say next time you catch yourself behind him at the water fountain.
COMMUNITY INVOLVEMENT/ VOLUNTEERING	Especially if you are civic-minded and shy, you won't find a better way to get to know someone than through a meaningful shared activity where the focus is not just "laserlike" on the two of you.
LETTER OF INTRODUCTION (FOR FOREIGN DIGNITARIES AND MEN LIVING IN THE 1800S ONLY)	You can write it and make it as flattering as you want, but just make sure a true notable signs it.

The Who, What, Where, and How of Meeting a Guy

PLACES WHERE YOU CAN MEET HIM	TIPS FOR MAKING THE PLACE HEAVEN INSTEAD OF HELL
WORK	If you don't have enough pain and anxiety in your life, choosing to date someone you work with is a sure way to fix that. You'll get that thrill from being illicit; after all, dating at the office is still a social taboo. But God help you when you have your first argument, need space, but find yourselves face-to-face at the watercooler.
BEACH	At least you won't have to wonder what he looks like naked. But just be aware that a piña colada-fueled flirtation is tougher to sustain once you are off the sand.
PERSONAL AD— WHAT WORKS AND WHAT DOESN'T	• Do tell the truth about yourself, with a focus on your best qualities. • Do require a picture before meeting. • Do talk to him on the phone before meeting. • Don't say anything that makes you sound desperate—e.g., "I am still searching for love" or, like a loser, "My last five boyfriends all dumped me. Will you be the one?"

TIPS FOR ON-LINE DATING: HOW TO DEVELOP A WINNING PROFILE!

Of all the different ways you can meet a man these days, on-line dating is the most compelling and popular social parlor of the new millennium. Chat rooms are a growth industry.

Just when you thought you had mastered the art of face-to-face interaction, now you need to learn how to present your self via computer. That means you need to get a photo of yourself taken, one that reflects how you look now, not at the prom. You need to find the sites and chat rooms that reflect your desires. And you need to create a profile. But how do you describe your sexy self in a nutshell?

You must develop a winning profile! Use the following top ten tips to create a winning profile that'll create a dating triumph instead of tragedy.

1. Don't lie much. Spell out who you are and what you want honestly. If you're obese, don't call yourself beefy. If you're sixty-five, don't say you're in your thirties. It's good to be specific, but for God's sake, keep in mind you are not an ATM. Don't sound too transactional.

2. Avoid Dorian Gray syndrome. Picture-swapping is the quickest way to get a man to respond to you. But make sure your picture is from the most recent decade. If your picture makes you look like you're twenty-five when you really look forty-five, either carry a red silk scarf for instant light dimming, or don't be surprised when you get a negative reaction.

3. Be Sharon Stone and trust your "basic instincts." If someone gives you the creeps after you have talked with him awhile on-line, just spare yourself a bad drink or dinner and move on. He won't be more interesting in person.

4. Don't be an HR statistic. If your company has strict policies about private Internet use, don't turn your PC into a downloadable version of *The Dating Game*. Save your man search for home, or you might end up paying for your dates from your unemployment check.

5. Remember Glenn Close! You are having a fun time talking, and before you know it, you have sent him your work telephone number once you have decided to meet him for at least thirty minutes at Starbucks, the standard, if unoriginal, minimum for an on-line date. Two dates later, your "fatal attraction" date seems unstable enough for you to send your bunny to Europe for the summer. Don't give him your work number, or even your home number, until you have gotten to know him better.

6. As time goes by, some things look the same. As the song goes, "You must remember this, a kiss is still a kiss," and a penis is still a penis. So before you send him a picture of your privates, remember that the chances of distinguishing yourself by sending a grainy, x-rated shot of yourself are slim. And if you are really looking to date, guess what image he'll have when he looks into your eyes during dinner.

7. Keep your expectations in check. Though on-line dating is a reasonable alternative for today's busy, professional gay male, it takes two wise men to overcome the inherent danger of unreasonably high expectations. After all, you have a vision in your head of Mr. Right, you see a wonderful, self-selected picture of someone from when he thinks he looks the best, and you are hearing all the greatest things about him (the moonlight talks and beach walks). Just remember that you are a real person with flaws meeting another real person with flaws.

8. Loose lips sink ships. It may be easy typing secrets to strangers during a weak moment when you are in a chat room, but think twice. Telling him about the men who never understood you, and the deep dark secrets that only your therapist knows, should be saved for much later in your relationship, preferably when you are on your deathbed after a long and happy life together.

9. Believe 50 percent of what you hear and none of what you read. It is healthy to be a little skeptical about people you might chat with on-line. Don't believe everything you read, and take profiles with an enormous grain of salt.

10. First meeting should be public. Don't meet him for the first time at your, or his, apartment, unless you are comfortable never seeing him again. No matter how much you talk about inviting him over to your place just to "hang out," make no mistake: it's a sex date. And sex dates are sex dates. Not that they can't turn into real dates, but you are playing a numbers game and the percentages aren't in your favor if you think you can turn a sex date into a dating relationship.

PART IV

Marking the Milestones of Gay Dating

Each step along the way is an important part of dating, whether it's meeting his friends for the first time or throwing a party jointly. As you climb *The Mandates* ladder of dating, remember that each step can take you higher or lead to your fall. Therefore, pay attention to what happens at each of these stages.

Here are tips for handling each new phase with strength, smarts, and insight. In this section, *The Mandates* explores the dos and don'ts for the first time each of the following occurs:

THE FIRST	DO	DON'T
Date	Be charming and mysterious. And follow *The Mandates*!	Go overboard in any aspect (e.g., flowers) that will throw the initial balance off.
Gift of flowers	Send him a card with thanks.	Call him crying, telling how this one act erases thirty years of heartache and pain.

THE FIRST	DO	DON'T
Date when you *don't* clean your apartment immediately prior to his arrival	Smile to yourself and don't let on that this is something you even thought about.	Tell him what a huge milestone this is for you, how this is indicative of your trust in him growing by leaps and bounds.
Time you meet *his* friends	Be friendly, easygoing but come off as nobody's pushover.	Hold on to him as if he were the last slice of bread in a famine, look around skittishly, and sullenly withdraw when you aren't the center of attention.
Time he meets *your* friends	Keep the conversation going by casually bringing up commonalities where they exist, so they will have a chance to get to know one another.	Act nervous and try to dominate the conversation any-time you think there's even the slightest chance that one of them might say some-thing you don't want them

THE FIRST	DO	DON'T
Morning after a sleepover	Make a great breakfast at your place, and clear your schedule so at least the first part of the day is devoted to being together.	Wake up like a fire alarm has just gone off and you need to slide down a pole to get the hell out of there.
Disagreement	Take a step back once you feel that you have heard him, and he has heard you. There's nothing wrong with some time to process a disagreement, but it doesn't mean you can't be decent to each other.	Bolt for the border just because you couldn't agree on which movie to watch or whether you told him the concert was Friday night, instead of Saturday.

THE FIRST	DO	DON'T
Time you see each other out at a bar/restaurant after you've started dating	Greet him like neither of you has any secrets and that it's great you are seeing each other, while being respectful of his time with whoever his companion is (if there is one).	Sit down at his table and crash his party, asking lots of questions about whom he is with and what he is doing, as if you are leading the great inquisition.
Joint vacation getaway weekend	Pack some special wine, or plan some special side trip to help make it memorable.	Keep discussing it with him as if everything depends on how you get along for this amount of time, reminding him it's the longest time you have spent uninterrupted.

THE FIRST	DO	DON'T
"I love you"s spoken	Just take in the moment, your surroundings, and what you are feeling.	Grab your hair in your hands, rocking back and forth, crying, "What does this all mean?"
Night you are busy when he wants to see you	Stick with your plans, but make a plan with him for the next available night.	Tell him he is a "frickin' ball and chain" and you can't take the pressure.
Night he is busy when you want to see him	Wait and see if he offers an alternative plan for the next available night; otherwise just tell him you hope you can see him soon.	Tell him he is a "frickin' Peter Pan" and you can't take the avoidance.
Party you throw jointly	Plan ahead so you agree on most points (number of guests, budget, date) before plans get too far under way to change or get out of.	Wait until the last minute and then bitch at the relatively higher number of guests he's invited and the amount of money he wants to spend.

THE FIRST	DO	DON'T
Time you meet his parents	Take a small gift and listen more than you talk.	Show up late, kick back a couple of cocktails before dinner, then make loud, inappropriate jokes as if you're at a Friars roast.
Sit-down talk about "the future"	Approach it like a partnership and something you'll discover together.	Come with a list of demands as if you were leading the SALT II talks.
Apartment or house you share	Be gracious about merging your styles and stuff.	Give him two shelves and a closet and fill the rest of the place with your things.
Dog you get together	Take the dog to training together.	Tell him you can't have sex anymore because "the dog will see."

Marking the Milestones of Gay Dating

THE FIRST	DO	DON'T
Piece of real estate in which you co-invest	Have a clearly written contract drawn up so that the rules of what happens to the property if it is ever sold are crystal clear.	Stick to the argument that since you both live there, "emotionally" it's a fifty-fifty investment, so you own half.
Pictures he sees of your old boyfriends	Tell him that he's better looking than all of them combined.	Fondle each one longingly and sigh as you sadly discuss how each relationship ended.
Time he meets your ex	Be friendly but make it clear who your new boyfriend is.	Introduce your boyfriend as your friend and start talking about the past.

PART V

Testing Your Understanding of the 25 Mandates

Are you ready to test your understanding and mastery of the twenty-five mandates? Everyone knows that dating can really test your patience. Before you go on one more date, take the following quiz and see how you react to common dating situations.

Add up the points accompanying your responses and then check the key at the end of this section to see how you rate!

1

You're at a bar and you run into the guy you've wanted to date for months now. Twice he has asked for your phone number. Twice you have given it to him. Twice you have gone home and perched yourself next to the phone like Pavlov's dog, waiting for him to call. Twice you have ordered pizza as a reaction to no phone call. He is friendly and solicitous. He looks great. He asks for your number again. He makes vague excuses for why he couldn't call. You:

a. Pull out yet another card and hand it over to him.
b. In a whiny voice, ask him if he's "really going to call this time. Really? You promise?"
c. Ignore the stack of cards in your right pocket and tell him you don't have any. Then ask him for his card in your most seductive voice. At the end of the evening, excuse yourself to the men's room and tape his card to the mirror.

d. Feel your pockets and then shrug. You ask for a pack of matches from the bartender. You ask to borrow a pen. You write down the name and number of the liposuction doctor whose name is on all the subway ads. You smile, pat his shoulder, hand him the card, and whisper in his ear that the third time is fate, before going to talk to someone else.

2 You're introducing the guy you're dating to friends for the first time. They bring up the weekend party last summer when you went a little wild and threw yourself at some hot man on the dance floor who ended up totally blowing you off. Before they can go further, you stop them by:

a. Pleading with them in a whiny, tiny voice to stop it.
b. Giving them a sharp look, but then you blow it by laughing nervously.
c. Circling the table with a pointed finger, telling something embarrassing about each one to cut them off at the pass.
d. Making light of it, acting nonchalant, and firmly changing the subject to something personally neutral yet provocative that will turn all attention on you.

3 It's the second date and the guy starts whining about his ex, droning on about how much he loved him and how awful it was to get dumped. You respond:

a. *Oh, that must have been rough. Lean on me. Let me be your strength.*

b. *The same damn thing happens to me. All the time. Men suck, don't we?.*

c. *Remind me again, what does this have to do with me?*

d. *You've obviously got some issues to work out. A first date isn't the place to do that.*

4 Before your dinner date with a hot, promising new guy, you meet him at his place for a quick drink. While he's getting drinks in the kitchen, you scan his CD collection. He has thirty-seven Barbra Streisand CDs, placed in alphabetical order, from *A (All About Barbra)* to *T (Timeless: The Last Concert)*. Superstud comes out of the kitchen with your vodka and cranberry and sees you rifling through his music. You quickly try to cover up your snooping by saying:

a. *I just love Babs's songs from the seventies the best! "Stoney End" rules!*

b. *I don't care what anyone says. Barbra may be better in the studio, but Liza wipes the floor with her onstage.*

c. *All I see for miles here are dance music and divas. Jesus, Mary, are you gay?*

d. *Okay, so how sacred is Babs before I admit to having seizurelike symptoms when I hear "You Don't Bring Me Flowers"?*

5 Your boyfriend of one month unexpectedly shows up for an overnight date with two duffel bags' worth of clothing and toiletries, which he dismisses as "just a few things I want to leave here in case I ever need them." This is the first time either of you has brought extra clothes and supplies to a date. What's the best thing to do?

a. Immediately clear out a closet as you weep with tears of joy.

b. Totally freak out and start flinging his undies and shave cream out the window.

c. Start packing your bag for his house.

d. Ask yourself how comfortable you feel with this, then respond honestly. Talk about what this means exactly in terms of your relationship.

6 You are about to have sex with a guy at his place, you both share your HIV-negative status, then he insists on barebacking with you. What do you say?

a. Sure, sounds fun. Last time I barebacked was at Camp Rancho Big Fun in Montana when I was eight.

b. Barebacking seems a little risky, right? But you are so cute and I am so lucky to have caught your eye!

c. No, doofus, I am not interested in risking my life for you or giving in to your demands.

d. Saddle up and trot on outta here, cowboy.

7 Your ex invites you to his commitment ceremony. What's the best gift?

a. Something from Tiffany! After all, it's his special day.
b. Your support and presence, showing how you have made peace with him and the cruel way he left you for this younger, insipid man he's now marrying.
c. Why are you going?!
d. Tabasco and Ex-Lax slipped into the au jus prior to delivery of London broil entrées prepared for the reception.

8 After six months, you and your boyfriend decide to be monogamous, only for you to find out after one year that he meant "as long as we're both in the same state." Your reaction?

a. Understanding. After all, you never clarified, did you?
b. Questioning. How could you have misjudged his intentions?
c. Unforgiving. He should have said what he wanted up front. He's backpedaling now to save his ass.
d. Resigned disappointment. Tell him that as far as you're concerned, he already is in another state. It's called denial. And that you are now in another state as well. It's called single.

9 You respond to a personal ad written by a guy who describes himself as six feet two, 185 pounds, brown hair, blue eyes, athletic, and thirty years old. He shows up for your date, but is gray-haired, wears Coke-bottle glasses, is bony and soft, and at least fifty. What do you say?

a. Hi, it's okay that you lied through your teeth. I am sure you are a nice person. Coffee?

b. You aren't exactly what I was expecting, but I guess these on-line dates are all about keeping expectations in check.

c. It's not that you're twenty years older than you said, or that you look undeniably different. It's that you lied to me. That's no way to begin either a friendship or a romance. Ciao.

d. Yo, Daddy! Where's your son, the one I was looking forward to meeting?

10 After a particularly bad affair, you decide to lower your standards so that the next one will last. Next thing you know, a mincing, bitter, frosty-haired manicurist named Irwin has moved in with you, filled your home with tacky, bejeweled tapestries, gilded International Male clothes, and cheap Target furniture. After three months, you:

a. Accept things as they are. Relationships are about compromise.

b. Tell him that you're cutting the Target credit card off if he doesn't ask you next time he charges $2,000 worth of crappy lawn chairs. Then you renege and make up with him.

c. Go into therapy ASAP. Keep asking yourself, "Who am I?" until the small, still voice within says, "You're an idiot."

d. Kick his mangy, tired, taste-free butt o-u-t.

11 You are on date with a guy who keeps popping little white tablets he calls "special breath mints" onto the tip of his tongue after dinner, as he gets increasingly more loving, friendly, and ethereal. He offers you one. You say:

a. Oh, thanks. A breath mint that makes me extra happy would be groovy.

b. That doesn't look like a Tic Tac. It's too round.

c. Do you want to watch the Valley of the Dolls video again?

d. Lying to me about your ecstasy pill-popping is so nineties.

12 You respond to an on-line personal and, after viewing a few pictures and talking a few times by phone, decide to meet the guy. But his pictures don't do him justice; in person, he looks like Brad

Pitt. Yes, you found the one-in-a-million guy who understated his attributes on-line. All of a sudden you feel panicky, so you:

a. Get really defensive and insecure while you're talking with him. You quickly excuse yourself, head to the men's room, and inject yourself with Botox.
b. Fawn, drool, and genuflect at his feet. Yep, that'll make you look so sexy.
c. Stop listening to what he says and imagine the two of you living on your dream ranch. You'll have plenty of time to get to know him later once the ranch is built and you've moved in together.
d. Treat him like you would anyone. Anyone you think is hot, that is. But keep your pride as you lose your hormonal balance.

13 It's been three blissful dates with your dream guy, but you've been placing all the calls, making all the exciting plans, and feeding your friends a minute-by-minute account of the romance that's blossoming in mind. Meanwhile, you only see him in public places, there's been nothing physical between you, and he's canceled twice at the last minute for vague reasons. Your next move?

a. Just keep making the moves. Not everyone is as organized as you!

b. Excuse his behavior by rationalizing to yourself that he's superbusy and has a really important career and social life, much more important than yours.

c. Realize that you're driving your "streetcar named desire" down a one-way, dead-end track.

d. Stop calling and making plans, then see what happens. As obvious as it seems, remind yourself that you only want to be with someone who likes you.

14 Everything is going great in your relationship until one day, after you've begun to feel comfortable with each other after a few months of dating, you are bored with him and the relationship for the first time. Your immediate reaction is to:

a. Wonder what it is that you've done wrong. Feel terrible about yourself.

b. Bolt out the gate like a Triple Crown winner.

c. Take a little time alone to examine the relationship and determine if there's something you want to (and could) change.

d. Tell yourself that it's natural in a healthy relationship to have an ebb and flow of desire. Trust that if things are generally good, this will pass.

15

On your eighth date with a guy you met at the gym, you discuss the whole "out" issue. Mr. Gym guy says that, yes, he's out at work "to a guy on the second floor." Asked if he's out just "in general," he responds, "Yes, definitely. I mean, I think so, I don't discuss it but I don't hide it. It'd probably surprise a lot of people. They know about the women but not the men." Finally, when you mention meeting some of your friends for dinner in the gay section of town next weekend, he avoids answering. What do you do?

a. Whisper that you'd be happy ordering in Chinese food alone with him forever, just the two of you.

b. Think to yourself how cool it is that he skipped being gay and went right to being the trendier "postgay."

c. Wonder if you should curb those burgeoning romantic feelings because you cannot deal with dating another "straight as a circle" confused case.

d. Tell him he's more closeted than last week's dry cleaning. Ask him if he agrees that a healthy relationship eventually needs to be integrated with family and friends.

a. 1 point

b. 2 points

c. 3 points

d. 4 points

ANSWER KEY

IF YOUR TOTAL SCORE FOR ALL FIFTEEN QUESTIONS IS:	THEN YOU ARE:
15-24	**A medical miracle.** How you have survived in the world thus far with no spine is a mystery to all who know you.
25-34	**Definitely dysfunctional.** You are a man in desperate need of discipline. Consider joining the air force and getting your wings for a brief two-year stint before flying with the self-esteem impaired.
35-44	**Hopeful hot–stepper.** Keep climbing! Your esteem is improving, but you need to keep taking those steps!
45-54	**Delightfully devilish!** You are not to be confused with malicious. Malicious is offensive in every sense of the word. Devilish just means you are your own best judge and defense. You can take care of yourself.
55-60	**Flawless.** You are a Mandates role model in the making.

PART VI

Competition! Managing the Inevitable Devil

(or what to do when it takes a village. . .to keep him hooked)

You are totally monogamous and want to keep the peace before either of you goes out and gets a piece. Or you are in an open relationship but you want to hold the cards and take out any jokers, princes, jacks, or wild cards (like the guy he meets on a business trip and decides he likes better). Or you are still at that interim stage where you are navigating the rocky waters of your relationship day to day, trying to keep it afloat, be a couple, make plans for the future, and yet not crowd that all-important male requirement—space. On a percentage basis, probably close to 80 percent of all gay male couples are in that "interim" phase mentally, if not historically or chronologically.

The male species has been fighting for individual space and the delineation of territory since Cain and Abel, so why pretend it won't happen, even if you are in the mushy phase of your relationship where you both walk on air? My advice in this stage is jump to earth before you get too high. It hurts when you're thrown to the ground.

For men subscribing to *The Mandates*, competition can enter into play early on in dating. That's why it's best to face it head-on and not be an ostrich, sticking your head in the sand as if it won't come up sometime soon. Just remember, ostriches have to come up for air eventually!

Here are some common situations in any gay dating relationship, and ways to deal with them effectively. They are enough to bring out the competitive jungle animal in any man.

COMPETITIVE SITUATION	THE MANDATES REACTION
He checks out another guy walking down the street/in a restaurant.	Smile and give him the old mock-cocked-eyebrow look that says, benevolently of course, "Two can play at that game, pal."
He's going on a business trip for more than five days.	Business events usually mean lots of pressure, with lots of unwinding thrown in at some local pub or restaurant. Hopefully, he works with the ugliest people you have ever seen. But if not, and you feel a twinge of anxiety, try to keep some routines. For example, call him at night before bed if that's something you normally do, but if he's not in yet, don't leave escalating, hysterical messages on the hotel machine.
His "wild" friend from his early coming-out days is flying in to see him for the weekend.	Just count on being excluded for at least 50 percent of all conversations, and try to include some of your new friends whenever possible for the requisite round of drinks

COMPETITIVE SITUATION	THE MANDATES REACTION
	and dinner, etc. Be charming and easygoing and give them some space alone, and you'll be rewarded later.
He's having dinner alone with his ex	Why aren't you going? Unless he's going for a "closure session" based on a messy breakup, I wouldn't be too happy about this unless they have long since established an easygoing, platonic friendship. If they have, I direct you back to my original question.
He plans a night out with his friends from the summer beach house he shared before you met him.	Plan a night out with a group of your friends as well. Every guy needs his nights out with buddies.

COMPETITIVE SITUATION	THE MANDATES REACTION
He plans a night out with his friends from the summer beach house he shared before you met him . . . *and that beach is Fire Island Pines.*	Okay, well, this is an exception that requires a little more strategizing. Most of these Fire Island beach boys have seen and done it all and might want to bring the bacchanalia to dry land for an evening. Try to figure out a way to go, without seeming desperate for an invitation. If nothing else, you'll learn a lot about his tolerance and appetite for the wild side of life.
You find out he has/had an on-line alter ego (review his list of screen names!).	Thanks to AOL, we are now a nation of "gay Sybils," with the potential for a different screen name for every mood and personality. If you find out that your boyfriend has maxed out the "up to seven screen names per account" rule of AOL, you might want to have a talk with him about what split personalities can do to relationships.

Competition! Managing the Inevitable Devil

COMPETITIVE SITUATION	THE MANDATES REACTION
You accidentally discover in his VCR a porno tape you have never seen before. Find out what he likes when no one's looking	Well, of course, you are going to watch at least some of it. Maybe this is a subtle way to find out new things he likes. Playfully try out a few of the film's lines at dinner one night, as in "Yeah, give me that stick of butter." See how he reacts.
Managing the crowds when you are having dinner at a gay restaurant in any of the following areas (Chelsea/NY; Castro District/San Francisco, CA; South Beach/Miami, FL; West Hollywood/Los Angeles, CA; P-town/Provincetown, MA)	Plan ahead for anything but a quiet dinner for two. What are the chances you'll run into someone one of you knows? Good. What are the chances you'll both be a little distracted by the crowds? Good. An old boyfriend of mine once said, "I can't help it. I get around crowds of gay men and my ears perk up like a dog's when there's new blood in the territory." Okay, but make sure you factor in quiet time for the two of you during trips to gay meccas.

PART VII

The Mandates
Role Models and
Spiritual Advisers

ROLE MODELS

●

Finding good gay role models is hard. After all, it is only in the nineties that gay male characters in movies were allowed to live, let alone date. In the fifties, gay male characters were offered up as sacrifices in film after film. In the sixties, they were allowed to live and be bitchy and wear purple. In the seventies, they were second and third bananas, full of comic relief. And in the eighties, of course, they all died of AIDS.

Finding role models is tough for heterosexuals, too, these days. But finding good *The Mandates* role models is even tougher.

When you look at the influential worlds of movie characters, acting, politics, music, books, celebrity, business, sports, fashion, and history, whom do you admire for their solid *The Mandates* sensibilities?

Here's a list of some individuals and characters who stand out and make us proud to be followers of *The Mandates:*

- **Rupert Everett in *My Best Friend's Wedding***

- **Russell Crowe's incredible gay son in *The Sum of Us***

- **Simmering and smoldering fashion leader and icon Tom Ford**

- **Will from *Will and Grace***

- **Christian Campbell's character in *Trick***

- **Billy Bean, the "out and proud" former pro baseball player**

- **Alexander the Great**

- **David on *Six Feet Under***

But then there are those individuals and characters whose behavior makes *The Mandates* required reading:

- **The guys on *Queer as Folk***

- **Nathan Lane's classic queen in *The Birdcage***

- **Gay writer Edmund White, whose trail of sad memories surely earns him at least one really great date**

- **The entire cast of *The Broken Hearts Club***

- **Jack from *Will and Grace***

- **All the tortured gay male characters in Merchant Ivory films except Maurice**

- **British writers Oscar Wilde, Joe Orton, and Quentin Crisp**

SPIRITUAL ADVISERS

Prayer is very much a part of the Mandates. Whom do you pray to for certain qualities? Just as some people pray to St. Christopher for travel safety, gay men need to pray to key individuals (mostly not saints, but there are exceptions). The following is the list of the Mandates' spiritual advisers and what aspect of life to focus on when praying to them:

• **Chad Everett,** the doctor from the 1970s television medical drama *Medical Center* for **health.** When you are not feeling well, who better than an awesomely handsome doctor with piercing blue eyes and a great tan to make it all better? (Youngsters unaware of Mr. Everett's powers may substitute George Clooney from the television show *ER.*)

• **Elizabeth Taylor** for **hope** and **courage,** for if ever there was a "Mother Courage," she's it, especially thanks to her AIDS charity work.

• **Doris Day** for **parking.** Did you ever notice that, in her television show in the early 1970s in which Doris drove to her office in downtown San Francisco every single day, the lucky bitch always managed to find a parking spot directly in front of her building?

- **Mary Haines** from the film *The Women* (played by Norma Shearer) for **longevity in troubled relationships.** She weathered the storms through infidelity, catty friends, and changing social mores. So can you!

- **Suze Orman** for **money** and **financial freedom.** There's nothing like a dame when it comes to making wise financial choices. Pray to Suze and listen for answers on how to curb frivolous spending!

- **Blanche Devereaux** (actress Rue McClanahan's character) from *The Golden Girls* for **beauty and sexuality as you age.**

- **The ghost of Greta Garbo** for an **air of mystery,** so you are not as see-through as that tacky nylon disco shirt you thought you looked so hot in last weekend.

- And especially in light of trying to find that perfect mate, you must always drop to your knees for the goddess and possible future saint **Cher**—you pray to Cher for any number of things but mostly for **relationships.** She understands.

She feels the same things you do. She is reflective about men ("Everything I know about men could fit on the head of a pin and you'd still have room for the Lord's Prayer.") She feels lusty and full of bittersweet longing. Just look at her videos. She also keeps some perspective on love ("Men should be like Kleenex. Strong, soft, and disposable").

That's why she is the patron saint of *The Mandates*. Since the sixties, Cher has amassed a song library that will speak to all your relationship needs. Just think of her songs. "Skin Deep" (with the immortal lyrics "I go skin deep. To the bone. SOS. I am in distress. Tonight"). "If I Could Turn Back Time." "Take Me Home." "I Found Someone." "We All Sleep Alone." "Strong Enough." "Song for the Lonely." And, of course, "Believe." ("Do you believe in life after love?" Well, do you? She does.) Who else captures our particular zeitgeist as well?

Remember to think about Cher every day. Why? Because she's thinking about you.

PART VIII

Sixteen Great Things about *Not* Dating Someone of the Opposite Sex

Everyone knows all about the great reasons to date members of the opposite sex. Parental approval. Societal benefits such as elaborate wedding gifts and tax breaks. It's a hell of a lot easier to deal with your social life in a work setting.

But what about the reasons to be happy that fate has determined that you were meant to lead a life of "his and his" towels in the bathroom?

1. You don't have to call him even if you say you will because, deep down, he understands that male thing about not calling when you say you will.

2. There is less concern about sex on the first date and whether he'll respect you in the morning. "Will you respect each other?" is the question. More likely you won't even remember to respect each other in the morning until the next afternoon, by which time you are both—separately—well into your day.

3. No biological clocks ticking in the background of your relationship. (Added bonus: if you are both over thirty, you'll get to experience "gay menopause," the male version of the biological clock, during which you feel just fine, but suddenly all the other gay men around you start treating you as if you were old.)

4. You don't have to pretend that you would never fantasize about something else during sex for fear of hurting her feelings.

5. Chances are you don't have to face her father and ask for her hand in marriage.

6. You get out of having to deal with PMS. (Chances are your boyfriend's moodiness will be consistent rather than monthly.)

7. You might just get along fabulously with your mother-in-law.

8. The aforementioned possibility of sharing clothes and doubling your wardrobe.

9. No going into debt over engagement and wedding rings.

10. No birth control issues.

11. New laws in some states that let you share work health benefits.

12. If you want to get married, your only alternative is . . . Canada! (Or maybe New England.)

13. You can attend "men's issues" support meetings together.

14. The worry your parents had that you would grow up and marry a girl of a different religion just somehow fade into the background.

15. You probably won't have child support payments from a previous marriage. Therefore, more disposable income for you.

16. Sneaking into the bathroom for quickies is so much easier to pull off without attracting attention.

Of course, there are definite cons as well. The top ten cons you might face in same sex dating include:

1. You are twice as likely to be attracted to one of his friends when you double date.

2. You get home after a tough day at the office only to realize that you both want a wife . . . really bad.

3. Male egos. Enough said.

4. The risk of contracting a sexually transmitted disease (STD) is higher.

5. Men cheat more. In a national survey one thousand straight men married less than a year were asked, "Have you cheated more or less since getting married?" Ninety-eight percent answered "yes." More or less, indeed.

6. Chances are you know his ex. Gay circles seem smaller.

7. The unattractive possibility that you'll show up at the same party wearing the same outfit, and the even more unattractive possibility that you share the same first name.

8. If he dishes you with his friends, his friends are probably a tougher crowd than hers would be.

9. Just try getting a hotel room with one bed when you travel to Italy or another country rich in religious oppression.

10. Finding out that, despite your hard-won, newfound self-esteem, you are still expected to like the following objectionable things:

- **Disco music in the morning**

- **The color lavender**

- **Rainbow beads, flags, posters, blankets, clothes**

- **The film *The Women***

- **Leather harnesses and whips as a fashion statement**

- **Staying out way too late and going to clubs at 2 A.M.**

- **Long, lingering close–ups of Barbra Streisand in her films**

- **Free weights**

- **Ecstasy (no, not the spiritual kind)**

- **Secondary smoke inundation**
- **Getting judged constantly by how you look and dress**
- **Calling men girls' names**
- **The kind of compulsive socializing Thoreau called "vain and useless"**

PART IX

Male Partnership— Are You Ready? The Final Frontier beyond the Mandates

How does that song go? "Love and marriage, love and marriage, go together like the word 'disparage.' " Actually, it's "like a horse and carriage." But it will be "disparage" unless you watch your step.

Somewhere in between the extremes of the first date and chairing the National Freedom to Marry Coalition, there's a wide array of partnership options to consider. It's fantastic when you find a man who is interested in the same level of dating as you. But it also raises a whole new series of questions. How do you spend your time together? How do you share once-sacred and -solo areas of your life such as your bank account? What do you go through as you say goodbye to being single? What are the negotiable versus non-negotiable essential qualities you want in a mate? What's the difference between cold feet and real doubt? Does he support you in finding your own interests? And, if you ever did get married, would you ever agree to love, honor, and . . . obey?! Doubtful.

TEN-QUESTION RELATIONSHIP COMPATIBILITY TEST

●

A re you really right for each other? Do the signs indicate
that he's best suited for life with a closeted Republican?
Or is his match a rainbow-bead-wearing circuit boy? Take
this relationship compatibility test with the man you're dating seriously. Compare results. Will you be surprised?

1. My idea of a perfect weekend:
a. *Going out after a long week at work, partying at gay
   clubs nonstop.*
b. *Not moving from my couch potato perch, surrounded
   by food, videos, and magazines.*
c. *Spending time at the gym, going to the movies, and
   seeing friends, but making sure my partner and I have
   time alone together.*
d. *Sitting in m4m sex chat rooms and surfing porn sites,
   seeing what I can get free.*

2. How often do you expect sex?
a. *Daily, otherwise I am a neurotic mess prone to cheat.*
b. *I don't care. Unless it's a special occasion, I'd rather
   read* Vanity Fair.

c. It isn't the number of times, it's the quality and the connection that matters.

d. Just from myself, or do I include my partner?

3. How important is fidelity to you?

a. As long as my partner comes home to me and doesn't embarrass us, I don't care what he does.

b. If he cheats on me, I'll take him down!

c. It matters a lot; it reflects the commitment and respect we share.

d. It's right up there with watching hockey on TV and wearing open-toed shoes.

4. How do you resolve differences?

a. I'm always right. He should know that by now.

b. I avoid conflict at all costs by calling 1–800–therapist, and letting the operator deal with him.

c. We talk them out, distill what's really important, then figure how to compromise.

d. I pray to Ares, the Greek god of war, then head into battle.

5. How do you feel about getting older?

a. I'm planning more plastic surgery than Siegfried and Roy combined.

b. I'm increasingly depressed about it. But with a regular

combination of Prozac and Botox, my doctor says I'll be able to look as numb as I feel.

c. I'll keep up gym visits, healthy eating, and limit intake of any harmful substances in order to look good, but hopefully I'll have a sense of humor, too. It happens to the best of us, if we're lucky.

d. Who? Me? I am not going to get older.

6. What's the worst thing you can imagine your partner doing?

a. Cheating on me.

b. Spending money from our joint account without telling me.

c. Letting himself go physically and mentally.

d. Bringing home strays, and I don't mean dogs or cats.

7. Do you want to start a family?

a. My circuit party family is all I ever need. Can't wait for the White Party family reunion in Miami!

b. I dislike taking care of kids and wouldn't want my own.

c. I still want a daddy; I don't want to be a daddy.

d. I can't imagine not having a child, especially now that it's easier for gays to adopt.

8. How important is it for you and your partner to be "out"?

a. Being out is totally overrated. It's not worth the risks.

b. Very! I want our house so full of rainbow flags, you'll think you landed at a Wizard of Oz fan convention.

c. I want my partner and me to be equally open with family and friends. Secrets and hiding are damaging to the relationship.

d. I want us to be out, but not too out. But I also want us to be in, but not too in. In other words, I waver and need someone who either shares or accepts my vacillation.

9. How important is it that you and your partner share the same religious views?

a. Not important at all, since I have none.

b. Very important. He has to hate the Catholic Church as much as I do.

c. We don't have to agree, but it's important that we respect and support each other's beliefs.

d. I want him on his knees every Sunday morning!

10. How do you feel about sharing money, such as joint bank accounts, stocks, and mortgages?

a. What's mine is his.

b. He's not getting his grubby hands on one hard-earned penny unless I dole it out to him.

c. It's okay with me as long as we share the same financial goals and behavior. For example, sharing a fund

toward buying a house is fine, but I wouldn't want
a joint account for incidentals. He's a compulsive
shopper.

d. *I'd rather just split everything with him fifty-fifty and*
   keep our accounts separate.

Before making a major commitment talk about every-thing—money, sex, children, career, religion, degree of out-ness, pets, friends, and hobbies. Find out everything you can about a mate. It is common when you start dating someone to get to know each other's stories, but it takes more probing questions to avoid blind spots about the most important matters.

For example, don't stand there with a frozen look on your face when he comes home carrying a kitten, when you are allergic to cats. If you thought living together meant you'd have dinner together every night at 7 P.M. and he consistently parties after work with friends and colleagues, you need to address it sooner rather than later. And if you can't stand the thought of ever sharing a bank account, tell him before he comes home with "his and his" checks.

Most important, learn from your own experiences on the frontlines of gay dating. It's not the mistakes you make that damage you so much as the mistakes you make twice.

If you decide you are ready for one of the biggest steps you can take with another man, the public affirmation of your partnership, you need to review the laws on same sex partnership in your neck of the woods. You'll want to review your state's laws as well as familiarize yourself with pending national legislation similar to the recent Same Sex Marriage Act. Commitment ceremonies can range from more traditional religious ceremonies that mirror a straight wedding, to simple celebrations with a few close friends and family. It's important to note that, no matter how important a commitment ceremony might be to you, such ceremonies still don't offer much in the way of legal protection. In the eyes of the state and federal government, you as a couple have no extra rights. For example, the newspapers are full of stories of gay partners who were unable to visit their loved ones in the hospital, or who lost their home because the partners' wishes weren't covered in a will. For more legal protection, until legal gay marriages exist in our country, you still need to register as domestic partners where you can, create and update airtight wills, and make sure your family of origin knows, in writing, your intentions with your home and estate. To the eternal dismay of all gay men, it ain't over once you've registered at Bergdorf Goodman and Tiffany.

Web sites like Gayweddings.com provide a ton of basic information about how to plan for both the legal aspects of a partnership and the practical aspects of a commitment ceremony, should you choose to have one. Support the gay community while you bask in the glow of love amid your nearest and dearest. It's not just a political statement or supportive to hire gay caterers and vendors. It's sound judgment. Can you imagine any group more suited to handle flowers, food, and décor?

A little bit of *The Mandates* should stay with you even after you've celebrated your fifth-year anniversary. It's harder to keep the flames of passion roaring once you are taking out the trash together, taking turns scrubbing the bathroom, and jointly paying bills. Here are a few ways to keep the flames burning:

• **Don't let frustrations build up.** Fighting big about little things can be good. It's the repeated, small aggravations that are bad. A wise man once said that a single blow does not fell relationships. Most are clubbed to death with soft rubber mallets, beating away at the little things.

Jeremy and Keith, from Orlando, have survived Keith's testicular cancer, the rejection of Jeremy's parents once they found out he was gay, and the death of two close friends. Overcoming these difficulties bonded them, but when it comes to cleaning the kitchen, they remain in an ongoing war that's lasted eight years. Jeremy's an anal-retentive neatnik. Keith wants to retain his independent and arbitrary clean-up schedule. The arguments progressed to the point that they were damaging the relationship, so they decided to focus on the major issues surrounding what seemed like a simple compromise. Jeremy faced the critical parenting that had turned him into a judgmental perfectionist. Keith examined his

rebellious, stubborn streak that stemmed from being stifled by his conservative, overbearing upbringing. Today, their relationship is better than ever because they took the time to figure out why they fought so hard over dirty dishes in the sink and spilled drinks on the countertops.

• **Maintain your private space.** As insignificant as it seems when you are so over the moon and can't get enough of your partner, maintaining private space once you're living together matters. Sell off stock, pawn collectibles, or take a second job! Do whatever you have to do to always have your own bathroom once you're together 24/7. Get two televisions if there's going to be conflict over who's watching what when. Respect private time when he wants to read or just be quiet. These elements were cited by the majority of couples interviewed for this book as keys to successful cohabitation.

• **Patience.** As my friend Joe once said as he faced a budding relationship with a man who vacillated between wanting committed partnership and freewheeling, party-boy freedom, "A gay relationship has more hurdles than a track meet." Those hurdles include fear, shame, self-esteem, need for independence, same sex competition, and the shortage of older, coupled gay role models to show us the way. Patience in a gay relationship means understanding the common issues gay men face as we transition from dating to a more serious partnership.

• **Make time for each other.** There's no way that the urgency to see each other that you had when you first met will remain. It may reappear on occasion, but chances are you'll take each other for granted given the work and personal demands of life. It's just human nature. So guard against its happening. The fitness experts tell you to schedule your workouts as you would a required meeting for work. The same is true for a relationship. Schedule a recurring date night with each other, one that can only be broken for emergencies.

• **Don't take each other for granted.** You will hear some of his stories over and over, as he will yours. It's easy to think you know everything there is to know about him, but you don't. Tom and Al have been dating for two years and were getting concerned that they were finishing each other's sentences and turning into their worst nightmare—a bored and boring, old married couple. Their fears subsided when Tom noticed that, at every party they attended or gave, he learned something new about Al. Someone would ask Al a question or a topic would arise, and new information, opinions, and observations poured forth. Just the knowledge that there's always more to be learned has helped Tom and Al avoid the fear of boredom in a relationship.

• **News flash! You won't always agree.** In the initial blush of romance, you spend times counting all the things you have in common with your new crush. You then recount them to your friends with a gush of energy. It's important to have that checklist of desirable traits you want in a mate. And it's only natural to run down the list, checking off the positive matches one by one, to reassure yourself that you are making a sound choice. But, just prepare now for the moment when there's a disconnect. You will not agree on everything with your mate. It's an unrealistic expectation that you should shed as soon as possible, to save you time and grief. Disagreeing doesn't make either of you bad, nor does it mean your relationship is built on sand. You have to decide those "deal breakers" that you need to agree on, such as fidelity or money, and then just agree to disagree on the rest.

Peter and Neil are a good example. They've been together three years and living together one. "Neil and I have completely different political views and music tastes," Peter, a sales executive in Maryland, told me. "Neil is a relaxed moderate and I am a hothead liberal. He likes classical music. I like the popular dance stuff. Neil stiffens up like a cornered cat if he hears Madonna or the Pet Shop Boys. Opera makes me semisuicidal. But on a day-to-day basis, I have never been happier with anyone. We have a wonderful life together, love each other in ways no one even knows, and enjoy people, travel, and working on our home. So we bought his-and-his headphones and we save heavy-handed political discussion for when we're out with friends."

• **Don't sweat the small gay stuff, and it's all small, gay stuff.** All romantic relationships are tough at times, but gay guys face challenges that elude our straight brethren. Looks and sex appeal still rule, and the most critical judges of gay men are gay men themselves. Despite the progress in gay civil rights, we still live and love in a world where gay relationships are often scorned, dismissed, and, in some places, illegal. There's not only an acceptance of gay men staying young and boyish, you could almost argue that there's an unspoken "Peter Pan" conspiracy for us to stay single with our dating options open.

Eric, a twenty-nine-year-old Web designer, described his budding relationship as "really healthy, until a bunch of meaningless crap obsesses me. [My partner] Sean and I are so happy together, but then I watch some gay TV show like Queer as Folk, *and all of a sudden, I get swept away by the focus on drinking, drugging, tricking, fashion, and bitchiness. I wonder what I'm missing."*

Despite the growing number of gay couples and families, a predominant hedonistic streak within the gay male community sometimes seems at odds with a more settled gay relationship. A healthy gay partnership can be a triumphant defeat of those unsupportive forces.

Epilogue

Hopefully, the commonsense guidelines and real-life examples in *The Mandates* will make dating more fun for you. That's the simple goal of this book. Have more fun with dating as you triumph over the surplus of options, target your best type, weed out losers earlier, and avoid preventable dating drama. If you wade through the different types of men, and the numerous places and ways to meet, you deserve to have more fun. In some cases, you should get a dating Purple Heart for bravery in the face of chaos, coffee dates, and cocktail conversation.

The good news of gay dating is that no one's forcing you down an aisle strewn with rainbow rose petals toward a cake with two grooms on top. Take advantage of the fact that we, as gay guys, don't have the same pressure to conform as our straight brethren. We don't live in a world as closeted as it was for gay men a generation or two ago.

What you could call "bad" news is that you must know the expanded gay dating options so you can control them, instead of vice versa. Learn what you can expect from today's gay dating whirl and you'll be in a far better position to get what you want. Armed with information and the wealth of experience from gay dating "war" stories, you're much more likely to beat the odds and thrive on the frontlines.

About the Author

David Singleton is the author of articles on pop-culture and entertainment, such as game shows and "The Social Relevance of Barry Manilow." He also co-founded the E-Zine, *E-Pop!*, devoted to pop-culture punditry with a satirical, personal take on pop-culture's people, places, and events. *E-pop!* published twenty-six issues from 1999–2000.

With a BA from the University of Virginia and an MBA/MA in marketing and journalism from New York University, Singleton has worked within the publishing industry for companies such as Time Warner,

Scholastic, and Bantam Doubleday Dell for the last four-teen years.

An eleven-year resident of New York City, he now lives in the nation's capital with his partner, his (hopefully) last and (definitely) best date.